The BRMP® Guide to the BRM Body of K

Other publications by Van Haren Publishing

Van Haren Publishing (VHP) specializes in titles on Best Practices, methods and standards within four domains:
- IT and IT Management
- Architecture (Enterprise and IT)
- Business Management and
- Project Management

Van Haren Publishing offers a wide collection of whitepapers, templates, free e-books, trainer materials etc. in the **Van Haren Publishing Knowledge Base**: www.vanharen.net for more details.

Van Haren Publishing is also publishing on behalf of leading organizations and companies: ASLBiSL Foundation, CA, Centre Henri Tudor, Gaming Works, IACCM, IAOP, IPMA-NL, ITSqc, NAF, Ngi, PMI-NL, PON, The Open Group, The SOX Institute.

Topics are (per domain):

IT and IT Management	Architecture (Enterprise and IT)	Project, Program and Risk Management
ABC of ICT	ArchiMate®	A4-Projectmanagement
ASL®	GEA®	DSDM/Atern
CATS CM®	Novius Architectuur Methode	ICB / NCB
CMMI®	TOGAF®	ISO 21500
COBIT®		MINCE®
e-CF	**Business Management**	M_o_R®
ISO 20000	BABOK® Guide	MSP™
ISO 27001/27002	BiSL®	P3O®
ISPL	EFQM	PMBOK® Guide
IT Service CMM	eSCM	PRINCE2®
ITIL®	IACCM	
MOF	ISA-95	
MSF	ISO 9000/9001	
SABSA	Novius B&IP	
	OPBOK	
	SAP	
	SixSigma	
	SOX	
	SqEME®	

For the latest information on VHP publications, visit our website: www.vanharen.net.

The BRMP® Guide to the BRM Body of Knowledge

Business Relationship Management Institute (BRMI)

Van Haren PUBLISHING

Colophon

Title: The BRMP® Guide to the BRM Body of Knowledge

Author: Business Relationship Management Institute (BRMI)

Publisher: Van Haren Publishing, Zaltbommel, www.vanharen.net

ISBN Hard copy: 978 94 018 0022 8
ISBN eBook: 978 94 018 0532 2
ISBN ePub: 978 94 018 0533 9

Print: First edition, first impression, February 2015

The information contained in this material is subject to change without notice.

Details of the range of materials published under the BRMI Banner can be found at: www.brminstitute.org

If you would like to inform us of any changes that may be required to this publication, please email them to info@brminstitute.org.

For further information on the Business Relationship Management Professional (BRMP®) professional development and certification program, please visit:
http://brminstitute.org/professional-development/businessrelationship-management-professional-brmp/

For further information on the BRMP® training accreditation,
please visit: http://brminstitute.org/accredited-brmitrainers-and-training-organizations/

Alternatively, please contact BMRI at:

Business Relationship Management Institute, Inc.
747 Third Avenue, 2nd Floor , New York, NY 10017
Phone: +1.888.848.3012
Email: info@brm.institute
Online: www.brm.institute

For any further inquiries about Van Haren Publishing, please send an email to:
info@vanharen.net

Foreword

Allow me to start by congratulating you on picking up a copy of this book. You made a great choice!

I have two reasons for this...

Reason one: It's now commonly understood that properly educated and prepared BRM professionals can provide extraordinary benefit to organizations that employ them to more effectively use shared service assets and to target those assets more directly to improve business and strategic performance. This book will provide you the information and assist in learning the use of new terms, tools, and techniques that you'll need to accomplish this.

Reason two: As you explore, study, and apply the insights presented on the following pages, you will also improve your business value and your career prospects. In reviewing the 70 topics to be covered in this book and the corresponding Business Relationship Management Professional course, you'll find that while they do address their BRMP purpose, as their primary goal, they will also help you acquire the softer and ever more important skills needed to:

- Communicate in business terms
- Be a better leader in the enterprise
- Negotiate your client ecosystem more effectively
- Introduce beneficial change
- Inspire your team
- Become invaluable to the success of your business partners and the service providers you represent

Both of these expected outcomes, by the way, are no accident.

By way of brief background, I know something about BRM business value as I've implemented BRM programs four times as a corporate IT executive and I know that the expertise of the BRMI founders and leadership team as BRM thought leaders, practitioners, authors and teachers was built over two decades.

BRMI didn't stop there, though.

When it's decided that something can be improved using a better involvement process (such as BRM), not much thought usually goes into making the transition something that goes beyond moving from a yesterday to a today perspective.

BRMI's BRMP course and the book you are now holding in your hands, however, set forth the framework on how we can introduce ever more beneficial change to realize tomorrows we all want to see.

So, please prepare to enjoy the BRMI learning experience before you and know that it has been carefully arranged to help you advance in your career, make it last, and make it count.

Al Kuebler

Al Kuebler was senior vice president and chief information officer (CIO) for the McGraw-Hill Companies, Alcatel-Lucent, AT&T Universal Card Services and Los Angeles County. He's also authored 46 articles for CIO magazine, Computerworld, Forbes, Reuters and other IT management publications and the Amazon bestselling book: "Technical Impact: Making your Information Technology Effective, and Keeping It That Way."

Al is a pioneer in implementing BRM programs for joint business-IT collaboration to improve business and strategic performance through more effective use of the strategic engine of the enterprise, the IT function, as the truly powerful and exciting resource it is.

Al has received eleven industry awards for IT innovation in customer service and, as a member of the executive team at AT&T, he received the Malcolm Baldrige National Quality Award presented by the US Department of Commerce, National Institute of Standards and Technology (NIST) and the president of the United States.

Al is also the founder and principal of Technical Impact.

D

Acknowledgements

Writing a book of knowledge in any discipline is an audacious task requiring enormous commitment and dedication from subject matter experts, content reviewers, editors, and other contributors. This edition of Business Relationship Management Professional Body of Knowledge is no different—it is made possible by collaborative hard work of many dedicated individuals. Our principal authors contributed countless hours of work to generously share their professional knowledge shaping and polishing every section and every diagram to make them as clear and accessible as possible.

Business Relationship Management Institute is forever grateful to Vaughan Merlyn, this edition's chief contributor, chief editor, BRMI co-founder and Chief Knowledge Officer, without whose indistinguishable enthusiasm, dedication, and incredible expertise this book and the BRM Interactive Body of Knowledge (BRMiBOK), one-of-a-kind interactive repository of BRM wisdom on which this volume is based, would not exist. We thank Sheila Smith, an expert on Transition Management and BRM, who contributed numerous articles in both areas. We hope that, as you read this book, you will benefit from Sheila's ability to clarify complex concepts and present them in an easy-to-grasp way as much as we did, while we collaborated with her on this project. We thank Stephen Plante, who generously contributed the golden nuggets of his professional insights to sections on business-provider relationship management and improvement and business value optimization. In addition to contributing content to a wide range of topics, Roy Youngman, provided architectural expertise, leadership and technical oversight of data governance and content development logistics making it possible for this volume to be born and evolve as a stabilized and carefully scrutinized subset of the more dynamic larger BRMiBOK.

This book would not be possible without Aaron Barnes, a seasoned BRM practitioner, co-founder and CEO of the Institute who, together with Dr. Aleksandr Zhuk, the Institute's co-founder and President, kept the Institute running assisting the editorial and contents development teams in every way possible and contributing bits of valuable insight along the way. We thank Glenn Remoreras, an expert BRM practitioner, passionate BRMI volunteer and leader, established blogger, and frequently published BRM role evangelist, for his suggestions, insight, and inexhaustible enthusiasm! We thank members of BRMI Leadership Team including Aaron Barnes, Mark Edmead, Peter Lijnse, Vaughan Merlyn, Steve Plante, Alex Skinner, Sheila Smith, Glenn Remoreras, Ivy Remoreras, and Dr. Aleksandr Zhuk, who spent considerable time and energy reviewing all the comments submitted through the BRMiBOK. We would like to recognize the leadership and expertise Peter Lijnse provided guiding our course structure and publication.

Our special thanks to Meriah Barnes for reviewing and editing the contents. We thank Wanda Washington of Wanda Washington, P.C. (w@wwatlaw.com, www.wwatlaw.com) for her expert help in all legal matters. We are grateful to Anna Zhuk for designing the cover page of this volume. We also thank all our members and subscribers whose numerous comments and generously shared insights helped to inform our thinking and improve our understanding of the concepts presented herein. Any shortcomings and omissions you might find are solely our responsibility.

Sincerely,
BRMI Team

Preface

One of the most intransigent and perennial challenges an enterprise faces is the alignment between their service providers and the business they serve. The so-called 'alignment challenge' is especially visible when the provider is an internal Information Technology (IT) organization. In these cases, the IT budget often represents somewhere between 4% and 20% of revenues—a significant business cost. But IT providers are not the only ones that suffer the 'alignment' challenge. Human Resources, Facilities, Finance, and other shared services providers struggle to demonstrate their value and relevance to the businesses they serve. And with alternate sourcing arrangements becoming an increasingly important aspect of business operations, the 'alignment challenge' is as real for external providers as it is for internal shared services.

The role, job and organizational capability of Business Relationship Management (BRM) has emerged as a powerful means to address the alignment challenge. BRM first surfaced in 1990's, with little fanfare, as progressive IT organizations established the role to strengthen their business relationships, and to drive value realization from IT assets and investments. It gained legitimacy in 2005 with ISO/IEC 20000 service management standard, and was reinforced with the release of ITIL v3 in 2007.

In spite of this formal recognition, the BRM role is difficult to establish and sustain. On the one hand, it must represent and satisfy demanding business partners, who always want more while often not really knowing what they want or how to justify that demand. It must also satisfy the needs of the provider organization, and the complexities and constraints under which they operate. BRM is a connector—forging productive connections between provider resources and their business partners. It is also an orchestrator between the provider organization and its business partners—orchestrating key roles, resources and capabilities to help stimulate, surface, shape and harvest business value. Finally, BRM is a navigator—guiding provider business stakeholders along the best path to realized business value.

But establishing credibility, building trust, clarifying shared goals and closing the alignment gap demands a rare set of competencies, strong relationship skills, and an ability to thrive in highly ambiguous and even turbulent environments. The effective BRM is equally at home with their business partners and with their provider stakeholders—equally comfortable with the language and context of the business and the provider domain. They have at their fingertips models, frameworks and techniques to clarify strategy, stimulate innovation, prioritize investments, marshal appropriate resources and help ensure that business transitions deliver the full value that was expected from them. They have superb communication skills, able to "read between the lines," to hear the unspoken and to influence and persuade without having direct authority.

Business Relationship Management Professional® (BRMP®) training and certification program is designed to equip those interested in Business Relationship Management with the foundation knowledge they need to be successful.

This document is intended to support your BRMP® training experience and help you prepare for the BRMP® certification exam. Everything you need to know to pass the exam is within these pages. The passion to learn and grow, and the courage to be a great Business Relationship Manager must be within your own heart. But we hope that what you learn through this training will inspire your passion and strengthen your courage.

Vaughan Merlyn

Chief Knowledge Officer

Business Relationship Management Institute

F

Table of Contents

H

Page Intentionally Left Blank

1. Introduction to the BRM Role

This book provides an Introduction to the Business Relationship Management (BRM) role, discipline and organizational capability.

The concept of Business Relationship Management Business (BRM) is related to and employs the techniques and disciplines of Customer Relationship Management (CRM). However, while CRM most often refers to a company's external customers, the BRM typically deals with a company's internal customers or an internal Provider's products and/or services.

While BRM has its roots in CRM, it has come to mean different things to different people—often depending upon the specific industry context. For example, in banking and finance, the Business Relationship Manager manages and maintains current business relationships and seeks new accounts. Banking BRMs are typically responsible for a portfolio of small to mid-sized businesses. In other industries, the label *BRM* has come to be an euphemism for *account executive* or even *salesperson*.

The most consistent (though limiting!) definition comes from the world of Service Management, and, in particular, IT Service Management. Frameworks such as the IT Infrastructure Library (ITIL) and standards such as ISO/IEC 20000 call out the Business Relationship Management role as it pertains to service management.

1.1. Terminology

Throughout the BRMiBOK we use the following terminology:

- We refer to the role as Business Relationship Manager (BRM). In practice, the titles used by BRMs vary considerably (e.g. Business Partner, IT Partner, Account Manager, Business Unit Manager, Business Integration Manager).

- We refer to the BRMs business customer/client as Business Partner. Again, the terms used to refer to the Business Partner vary in practice (e.g. Customer, Client, Consumer).

- We refer to the Supply Organization as Provider. The Provider is most often an Information Technology organization, but increasingly BRM roles are being established for Human Resource, Finance, Training, Facilities and other enterprise functions.

1.2. BRM as a Role, a Discipline and an Organizational Capability

Business Relationship Management embodies a set of competencies (knowledge, skills, and behaviors) that foster a productive, value-producing relationship between a Provider organization and their Business Partners. These competencies can be leveraged through organizational roles (for example, in an IT Provider, the CIO typically has a role of BRM for the enterprise), a discipline (for example, all Business Partner-facing Provider roles should be skilled in Business Relationship Management), and an organizational capability (for example, a Provider organization should be effective in shaping and channeling demand to the highest value opportunities).

1.3. BRM Metaphors

The metaphors for Business Relationship Management (*Connector, Orchestrator,* and *Navigator*) can be helpful ways to think about and describe the BRM role, discipline, and organizational capability.

Metaphors can be a helpful way of describing a concept. We use three metaphors to describe the BRM role, discipline, and organizational capability.

1.3.1. BRM as a Connector

The BRM acts as a *connector* between the Provider organization and its Business Partners—forging productive connections between Provider resources and the Business Partner, and among Business Partners. There are three primary aspects to the BRMs role as a connector:

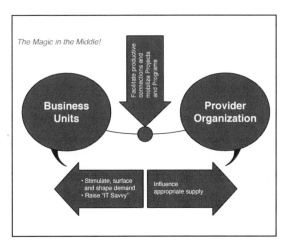

Figure 1 - The BRM as a Connector

1. Facilitate productive connections and mobilize projects and programs.

2. Stimulate, surface, and shape business demand for the Business Partner while increasing the *savvyness* within the Business Partner regarding the Provider's services and products.

3. Influence the Provider to ensure appropriate supply of services and products, both in terms of quality and capacity.

1.3.2. BRM as an Orchestrator

The BRM also acts as an *orchestrator* between the Provider organization and its Business Partners—orchestrating key roles, resources, and capabilities to help stimulate, surface, shape, and harvest business value. There are three primary aspects to the BRMs role as an orchestrator:

1. Orchestrate capabilities to drive value from Provider services.

2. Coordinate and aggregate business demand for the Business Partner.

3. Orchestrate key Provider roles on behalf of the Business Partner (e.g. Enterprise Architecture, Subject Matter Experts, Project Managers, and Program Managers.)

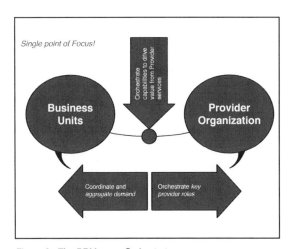

Figure 2 - The BRM as an Orchestrator

1.3.3. BRM as a Navigator

The BRM also acts as a *navigator* between the Provider organization and its Business Partners—navigating both the Business Partner and the Provider along a path to realized business value. There are three primary aspects to the BRMs role as a navigator:

1. Facilitate convergence between Provider and Business Partners. Convergence breaks down walls and embeds Provider capabilities within the Business Partners so as to increase agility and business value.

2. Facilitate business strategic planning and roadmapping for the Business Partner.

3. Guide key Provider roles on behalf of the Business Partner such as Enterprise Architecture, Portfolio, and Program Management.

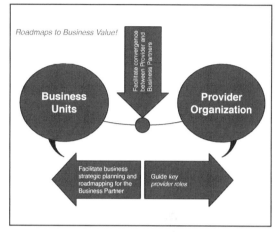

Figure 3 - The BRM as a Navigator

1.4. BRM-Related Standards

The BRM role is referenced in several industry standards, mostly associated with Information Technology, Service Management and the IT Profession. These include ITIL, COBIT, ISO/IEC 20000-1:2011, and the SFIA skills framework.

1.4.1. Background

It would be extremely helpful if there were meaningful standards associated with the Business Relationship Management role and profession. Unfortunately, today there are no such standards, though the BRM role is called out in some Service Management standards, is briefly mentioned in the COBIT business framework for the governance and management of IT, and is addressed in the SFIA skills framework.

It is an aspiration of BRMI, in collaboration with relevant standards-setting bodies, to help shape and establish meaningful BRM standards over time.

1.4.2. Purpose

BRM standards could help bring consistency and uniformity to the BRM role and associated processes. The downside is that insofar as such standards limit the role inappropriately, or fail to keep up with advances in the state of practice, such standards could constrain the growth and value of the BRM role.

It is the purpose of this section of the BRMiBOK to help BRMs be aware of related standards.

1.4.3. Current List of BRM-Related Standards

- COBIT—COBIT provides managers, auditors, and IT users with a set of generally accepted measures, indicators, processes and best practices, to assist them in improving the benefits derived through the use of information technology, and developing appropriate IT governance and control in a company.

- ISO/IEC 20000—ISO/IEC 20000-1:2011 is a service management system (SMS) standard. It specifies requirements for the service provider to plan, establish, implement, operate, monitor, review, maintain and improve an SMS. The requirements include the design, transition, delivery, and improvement of services to fulfill agreed service requirements.

- ITIL—ITIL (IT Infrastructure Library) is an approach to IT Service Management that embodies a framework for identifying, planning, delivering and supporting IT services to the business.

- SFIA—The Skills Framework for the Information Age (SFIA) is a system for IT Professionals to match the skills of the workforce to the requirements of the business. It is a logical two-dimensional skills framework defined by areas of work on one axis and levels of responsibility on the other. It has been proven as an effective resource that benefits business by facilitating all aspects of the management of capability in corporate and educational environments.

2. Organizational Capability

Business Relationship Management is an organizational capability. Every group in a service provider will have a relationship with the business (customers). In this chapter the organizational capability is discussed. The following topics are addressed:

- Capability Model
- BRM Core Disciplines
- Operating Model
- Business Provider Maturity Model
- Business Relationship Maturity Model
- Business IT Alignment

2.1. Definition of Business Relationship Management

Business Relationship Management stimulates, surfaces, and shapes business demand for a provider's products and services and ensures that the potential business value from those products and services is captured, optimized and recognized.

2.2. Capability Model

2.2.1. Framework for the BRMI Provider Capability Model

The BRMI Provider Capability Model uses a Capability Model framework to represent a set of related capabilities that is an extension of a Value Chain Analysis approach popularized by Michael Porter. This model represents the major capabilities any organization would need to have in place where there is a business generating demand for products and services and a Provider trying to meet that demand.

This framework also uses the technique of decomposition, which allows each higher-level capability to serve as the context for a more granular set of capabilities. The decomposition progresses down until the underlying processes are discovered at the lowest level of decomposition. In this way, the reader can progress from a higher abstraction of capability to a lower level of abstraction as needed with a clear understanding of the context of each capability.

It may be tempting to think of Business Relationship Management (BRM) as a *process* in its own right. But that would be confusing the *means* as an *end*. As an organizational capability, BRM is the means for achieving the highest value possible for services provided to a business by a provider, either internal or external. Therefore, BRM must exist within the context of how a business generates demand for those services and within the context of how the Provider meets that demand.

The BRM Body of Knowledge (BOK) sets this context by modeling a set of *normative* Capabilities involved in the shaping of demand and a set of *normative* Capabilities involved in satisfying that demand.

2.2.2. Putting BRM in the Context of a Provider Capability Model

The question is often raised: Is BRM more of an art or more of a science? Unfortunately, this question assumes that art and science are two ends of a continuum, which is not really the case, at least not for BRM. There are some aspects of BRM that can be ordered and structured into well-defined best practice processes much like any business process. There are other aspects of BRM that require dynamic judgement calls from people with an extensive amount of competence and experience. But even that competence can be defined as well as the process of increasing the level of needed competencies. In the end, Business Relationship Management requires a combination of defined processes and competent experienced people.

Accordingly, the BRM Body of Knowledge (BOK) is set into the context of Capabilities, which incorporates both the definition of best-practice processes as well as the standardization of needed competencies in people (and how to increase the level of those competencies). So in this sense, BRM is an art because there is a significant amount of judgement required that cannot always be prescriptive. Like artists, BRMs have to gain a high degree of competency to be effective. But BRM is also a science, because there are proven methods that can be applied based on commonly experienced situations.

BRM is a connector, orchestrator, and mutual navigator for a business that places demand for shared-services and the Provider that tries to service that demand. This means whether an art, a science, or a combination of both, BRM exists in the context of the interaction between DEMAND and SUPPLY. Therefore, BRM needs to be completely integrated with the business processes that generate demand and the Provider capabilities for servicing it. To meet this need, the BOK uses normative Capability Models following the framework described on this page for the key shared services to set the context of BRM. Since the BOK is focused on BRM, we include the breadth of all capabilities for a normative Provider with a perspective of BRM implications, and we add depth to capabilities that are BRM-intensive. The top-level normative capability model is the BRMI Provider Capability Model.

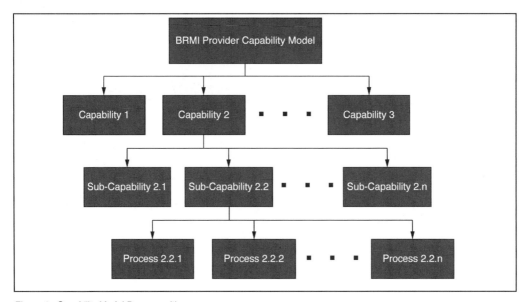

Figure 4 - Capability Model Decomposition

2.2.3. Basic Framework Design

There are two main types of content that serve as the building blocks of the overall BRMI Provider Capability Model: Capabilities and Processes.

- A Capability is everything it takes, both visible and behind the scenes, that makes producing goods or providing a service possible. This includes having people with the right competencies to play the roles required by defined processes, and armed with useful techniques and tools, all backed by management systems that create incentives for performance and improvement.

- A Process outlines a structured set of activities designed to accomplish a specific objective. A process takes one or more defined inputs and turns them into defined outputs. A process may reference any of the roles, responsibilities, tools, and management controls required to reliably deliver the outputs. Processes describe *what* to do whereas Techniques specify *how to do it*.

- Every Capability page has a graphical model that depicts its sub-capabilities or its processes (see Figure 4). Using the decomposition technique, a Capability may be composed of other sub-capabilities which in turn may be composed of other *sub-sub-capabilities* and so on. Each Capability has its own page in the BOK. The decomposition continues until reaching the point that further decomposition has little utility or actually insults the intelligence of our readers. The lowest level of granularity of this decomposition is called a *Process* rather than a *Capability* to distinguish the activity-oriented nature of reaching the lowest level of detail; therefore, Capability and Process pages differ in their content.

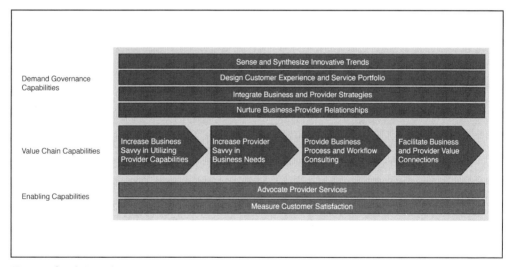

Figure 5 - Capability Model

2.2.4. Capability Descriptions

All Capability pages in the BRMI Provider Capability Model have a set of standard components designed to clarify the purpose, scope, and meaning of the capability and the implications the capability has on the Business Relationship Management discipline.

2.2.5. Capability Model

The first and key element of every Capability page is a graphical Capability Model.

A Capability Model is a collection of sub-capabilities or processes that work together for a common purpose. That purpose sets the overall context of the Capability and also identifies the end customers, who receive value from the collection of Capabilities. Please refer to Figure 5, as a sample Relationship Management Capability Model, and notice that the Capabilities are organized into three tiers:

1. At the core of a Capability Model is the value chain—those capabilities that create value based on the context of the Capability Model and its customers. If the context of the Model is the entire business, than the capabilities depicted in the value chain should create value to business customers. If the context of the Model is another high-level capability, than the capabilities depicted in the value chain should create value to whoever is a customer of that higher-level capability. This framework forces a discipline of thinking first about who the customers are and what really creates value in their eyes and is a key reason this framework was chosen to be the standard for the BOK.

2. Depicted above the value-chain capabilities are Demand Governance Capabilities—capabilities that are needed to manage the demand that flows into the value-chain. Shaping Demand is a core discipline of BRM which is another key reason this framework was chosen to be the BOK standard.

3. Depicted below the value-chain capabilities are Enabling Capabilities—capabilities that are needed to enable the value-chain or demand governance capabilities. Enabling capabilities are infrastructural by nature. They are essential and critical to success, but don't in themselves actually create value to the customers of the Capability Model. Separating them into their own tier helps reminds us what is the "end" (what value is created) versus what is a means to the end.

2.2.6. Example Relationship Management Capability Model

Understanding the differences between a value chain, demand management, and enabling capability is useful. It puts emphasis on what creates value and for whom that value is created. It builds an understanding that value chains consume resources and therefore need the ways and means to direct those resources to the highest value producers. Finally, these differences draw attention to the logistics that make it all happen, but in a manner that identifies it as the means to an end and not an end in of itself.

2.2.7. BRM Aspirations and Measures

Following the Capability Model on each Capability page, we start to focus on the BRM perspective of the Capability. First up is a list of business relationship aspirations which can be thought of as what a BRM should want out of the Capability. For each aspiration, there may be some metrics listed that could be useful measures of whether or not the aspiration is taking place. The main purpose of this section is to help BRMs consider the reasons they might care about any specific Capability, what they might want, and by what measure they would objectively know if that is happening.

2.3. BRM Core Disciplines

There are a few disciplines that are always in play when dealing with the dynamics of demand and supply with the goal of maximizing realized business value. These disciplines are considered for each and every Capability to provide a BRM perspective on each capability no matter what its focus or purpose.
The BRM Core Disciplines are:

- **Demand Shaping**—The Demand Shaping Discipline stimulates, surfaces, and shapes business demand for Provider services, capabilities, and products. It ensures that business strategies fully leverage Provider capabilities, and that the Provider service portfolio and capabilities enable business strategies. Most importantly, Demand Shaping is focused on optimizing the business value realized through Provider services, capabilities and products—that low-value demand is suppressed while higher value demand is stimulated.

- **Exploring**—The Exploring Discipline identifies and rationalizes demand. Business Relationship Management helps sense business and technology trends to facilitate discovery and demand identification. Exploring is an iterative and ongoing process that facilitates the review of new business, industry and technology insights with potential to create value for the business environment. The key benefit of this discipline is the identification of business value initiatives that will become part of the Provider portfolio of services, capabilities and products.

- **Servicing**—The Servicing Discipline coordinates resources, manages Business Partner expectations, and integrates activities in accordance with the Business Partner-Provider partnership. It ensures that Business Partner-Provider engagement translates demand into effective supply requirements. Servicing facilitates business strategy, Business Capability Roadmapping, portfolio and program management.

- **Value Harvesting**—The Value Harvesting Discipline ensures success of business change initiatives that result from the exploring and servicing engagements. Value harvesting includes activities to track and review performance, identify ways to increase the business value from business-Provider initiatives and services, and initiates feedback that triggers continuous improvement cycles. This process provides stakeholders with insights into the results of business change and initiatives.

Note that the Demand Shaping Discipline is performed primarily through Demand Governance Capabilities, the Exploring Discipline is performed primarily through the Value Chain Capabilities, the Servicing Discipline is performed primarily through the Value Chain Capabilities, and the Value Harvesting Discipline is performed primarily through the Value Chain Capabilities.

One or more of the BRM Core Disciplines are usually needed for any capability to perform effectively. For every Capability, we consider what aspect of each BRM Core Discipline is needed to make the Capability possible. Some capabilities will require more of one BRM Core Discipline than another, but we use the BRM Core Disciplines as a template for asking BRM questions when analyzing the application of the BRM Core Disciplines on each and every capability. Figure 6 provides a template of the most general questions as an illustration:

		BRM Core Disciplines			
		Demand Shaping	**Exploring**	**Servicing**	**Value Harvesting**
Capability Types	**Demand Governance Capabilities**	• How does demand enter into the value chain in the form that has the greatest chance of realizing value in the end? • How are decisions made when demand exceeds supply?	• What demand is not on the radar but should be? • How much can get invested in explorations and how are those decisions made?	• How do service consumers and customers become more savvy in the use of the value chain capabilities?	• How are leaks in the value chain identified and patched? • How do business stakeholders understand and perform their roles in realizing value?
	Value Chain Capabilities	• How are demand changes dealt with after that demand has entered the value chain? • How do those who create demand become more savvy in the potential value of Provider services and initiatives?	• How does high-level demand get broken down into workable alternatives and how is an alternative selected?	• How does the Provider of value chain capabilites become more savvy in the full purpose and implications of the demand they service?	• How does an organization become resilient to changes that are necessary to realize value?
	Enabling Capabilities	• How is the backlog of demand tracked?	• How can innovation coexist with ongoing operations?	• What levels of Provider services maximize business value and how should those services be bundled?	• How is value measured and monitored?

Figure 6 - BRM Core Disciplines

2.4. House of BRM

The House of BRM is a graphical representation intended to convey key aspects of a successful Business Relationship Management role, discipline, and organizational capability.

The House of BRM illustrates three key aspects of Business Relationship Management as follows:

- The *foundation* supports the BRM role and ensures it has the Competencies to be effective and deliver value to both the Provider organization and its Business Partners.

- The *pillars* define the BRM space in terms of BRM Core Disciplines—Demand Shaping, Exploring, Servicing, and Value Harvesting.

- The *roof* of the House of BRM protects Business Relationship Management as a key aspect of Provider capability. It does this by ensuring clarity around how the role, discipline and organizational capability of Business Relationship Management in the context of the Provider Strategy and Operating Model.

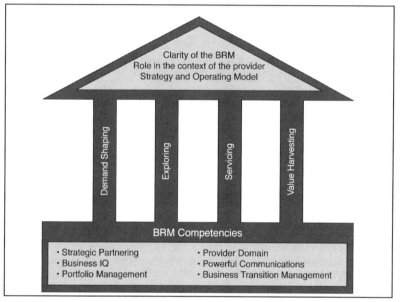

Figure 7 - House of BRM

2.4.1. BRM Core Disciplines

Business Relationship Management depends upon four Core Disciplines:

- *Demand Shaping*—The Demand Shaping Discipline stimulates, surfaces, and shapes business demand for Provider services, capabilities, and products. It ensures that business strategies fully leverage Provider capabilities, and that the Provider service portfolio and capabilities enable business strategies. Most importantly, Demand Shaping is focused on optimizing the business value realized through Provider services, capabilities, and products—that low-value demand is suppressed while higher-value demand is stimulated.

- *Exploring*—The Exploring Discipline identifies and rationalizes demand. Business Relationship Management helps sense business and technology trends to facilitate discovery and demand identification. Exploring is an iterative and ongoing process that facilitates the review of new business, industry, and technology insights with potential to create value for the business environment. The key benefit of this discipline is the identification of business value initiatives that will become part of the Provider portfolio of services, capabilities and products.

- *Servicing*—The Servicing Discipline coordinates resources, manages Business Partner expectations, and integrates activities in accordance with the Business Partner-Provider partnership. It ensures that Business Partner-Provider engagement translates demand into effective supply requirements. Servicing facilitates business strategy, Business Capability Roadmapping, portfolio and program management.

- *Value Harvesting*—The Value Harvesting Discipline ensures success of business change initiatives that result from the exploring and servicing engagements. Value Harvesting includes activities to track and review performance, identify ways to increase the business value from Business-Provider initiatives and services, and initiates feedback that triggers continuous improvement cycles. This process provides stakeholders with insights into the results of business change and initiatives.

2.5. Operating Model

Business Relationship Management is a component in the overall operating model of the Service Provider.

A Provider Strategy describes the Provider Mission, Vision, Strategic Intents, Outcomes, Values, Principles, and Policies. A Provider Operating Model is an abstract representation of how an enterprise manages its Provider resources and assets in order to deliver against its Strategy, including Governance, Services, Processes, Organization, and Metrics. The linkage between these Strategy and Operating Model components are important to the Provider's ability to deliver business value.

Operating Models should be designed with the Provider Strategy in mind. The Operating Model must support the strategy.

2.5.1. Not Just About the Provider Organization

While Provider organizations have traditionally been chartered with most of the primary responsibilities for management of a specific domain (e.g. Information Technology), the role of business executives, users and even end consumers is becoming important. Ultimately, value from Provider investments is realized within the business units and with external stakeholders. As such, a Provider Operating Model must address the enterprise and its ecosystem of vendors, partners, and customers—not just the responsibilities of those within the Provider organization.

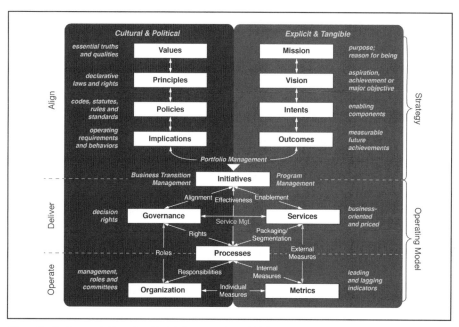

Figure 8 - Strategy and Operating Model. Components and Linkages.

2.5.2. Major Operating Model Components

An Operating Model is an abstract representation for how an organization utilizes its resources to create value. There are many ways to describe an Operating Model, but the major components typically include:

- Processes which require Roles that have specific Competencies in order to create Deliverables.
- Initiatives that are deployed in response to Strategy through the Operating Model.
- Organization structures which coordinate Roles and organize Resources and can include:
  - Service Centers for delivering routine, standardized "core" services and products for the enterprise such as an IT Operations Organization
  - Competency Centers to bring focus to a given competency (for example, Business Intelligence) and help transfer that competence to the broader organization
  - Integrated Solutions Centers comprising multiple disciplines and capable of delivering complex solutions such as solution development
- Metrics which measure:
  - The customer experience and service levels associated with Services
  - The performance of Processes
  - The success of a group as defined by its Charter
- Services defining the customer interface points of Provider Processes including services provided to business customers and, in some cases, end consumers, as well as those provided to other organizational units.
- Governance which allocates decision rights and provides the structures and process to enforce those rights.

RACI Charting

One of the results of an Operating Model is a RACI Chart.

A RACI Chart is a matrix of responsibilities that is especially useful in clarifying *who is supposed to do what* across an organizational setting. A RACI chart can be used to establish clear accountability for the performance of a process, or clear accountability for the making of a decision.

The elements of a RACI chart are:

- R — Responsible: *The doer*. A role that participates in an activity and is responsible for action or implementation. Responsibility can be shared.

- A — Accountable: *The buck stops here*. A role that *owns* the result of a decision—includes yes/no authority and veto power. Note: Only one role can be accountable, but sometimes that *role* can be performed by a body such as a governance board.

- C — Consulted: *In the loop*. Roles that have a particular expertise they contribute to a decision (i.e. their advice will be sought) or that must be consulted for some other reason before a final decision is made. Involves two-way communication.

- I — Informed: *Keep in the picture*. Roles that are affected by an activity/decision and therefore need to be kept informed—either kept up-to-date on progress or after the final decision is made or actions are taken. Involves one-way communication.

Role	Multi-year Strategy	Ideation	Analysis	Design	Testing	Maintenance & Operations	Value Optimization
BRM	R	A	A	C	C	I	R
Business Partner	A	R	R	C	R	C	A
Enterprise Architecture	R	C	R	C	I	C	C
Solution Delivery	I	C	R	A	R	C	I
PMO	I	I	R	R	R	I	I
Infrastructure / Operations	I	I	I	I	A	A	I

Responsible - "The doer"

Accountable - "The buck stops here"

Consulted - "In the loop"

Informed - "Keep in the picture"

Figure 9 - RACI Chart Example

2.6. BRM and the Service Provider

Any time the BRM organizational capability is introduced, there will be inevitable implications for other Provider roles and capabilities. If BRM and its implications are not re-calibrated and clarified, Business Relationship Management will be confusing, both to members of the Provider organization and to its Business Partners.

Therefore, the organizational capability must be clarified in the overall Provider Strategy and Operating Model context:

- What is the Provider Strategy and how does Business Relationship Management contribute to creating and delivering against that Strategy (e.g. Ensure integration between Business Partner and Provider strategies)?
- What Services does the Provider deliver to the business and what are the implications for Business Relationship Management (e.g. Strategy Roadmapping; Process Innovation)?
- What Capabilities does the Provider need to deliver those services and what are the implications for Business Relationship Management (e.g. Discovery & Innovation; Solution Delivery)?
- What Processes does the Provider need for effective Business Relationship Management capabilities (e.g. Portfolio Management; Project Management)?
- What Competencies do the Provider's processes require for effective Business Relationship Management capabilities (e.g. Business Analysis, Information Architecture)?
- What Technologies do the Provider's processes require for effective Business Relationship Management capabilities (e.g. prototyping tools, document management systems)?
- How are the Provider's capabilities Sourced and what implications does the sourcing model have on Business Relationship Management capabilities (e.g. In-house, Outsourced, or Brokered)?
- How are the Business-Provider relationships Governed? (e.g. Enterprise Governance Board, Portfolio Review Board)?
- How are the Provider's capabilities and Business Relationship Management effectiveness measured (e.g. Business Value, Service Availability)?

2.7. Business-Provider Maturity Model

The Business-Provider Maturity Model is a way to help surface and understand the growth in maturity of business demand for Provider services and capabilities, and a Provider organization's maturity of supply capabilities needed to both satisfy and shape that demand.

The Business-Provider Maturity Model employs an S-shaped learning curve to represent the growth in business learning to exploit the Provider capabilities and assets and the Provider learning to become efficient and effective in delivering services and, especially as maturity increases, shaping business demand. Business executives often find the model's simple elegance appealing. They quickly grasp the concepts behind business demand maturity and are able to use the model to analyze how their demand maturity is evolving over time. This equips them to engage in meaningful dialogue with Provider leadership about the business implications of both demand and supply maturity.

2.7.1. Background

The Business-Provider Maturity Model was originally developed in the early 1990s as the Business-IT Maturity Model (BITMM). It was developed by Vaughan Merlyn and a team of researchers he was leading at Ernst & Young's Center for Business Innovation. The model came out of a 3-year longitudinal study of 35 global IT organizations that were in various stages of IT organizational transformation. Vaughan subsequently led other

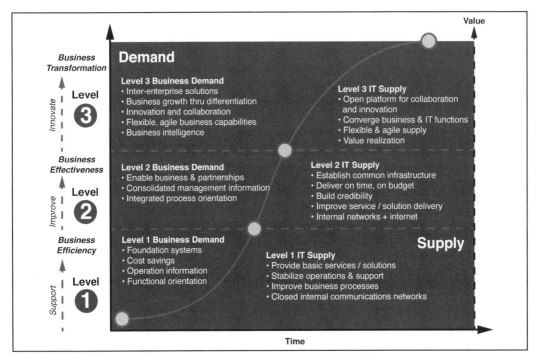

Figure 10 - Business - Provider Maturity Model

research teams at The Concours Group to further study and refine the BIMM, including the collection of detailed assessment data from about 100 global IT organizations. The model has also benefited from 20 years of practical application in the course of IT management consulting.

The research revealed that, while process management (the basis of CMMI) is a critical discipline, especially at low Business-IT maturity, reaching higher maturity requires sophistication with demand-side disciplines. For example, it is essential that strong business-IT relationships be forged and *IT savviness* be developed among business executives and users, especially about the business value of IT and what it takes to realize that value.

For these reasons, the Business-Provider Maturity Model addresses the maturity and trajectory of both business demand for the Provider's services and/or products (the business's *appetite*) and Provider supply (the ability to satisfy that demand)—*two sides of the coin*, as it were. In so doing, the model reveals patterns of inter-dependencies and disconnects between demand and supply over time. Demand and supply in many ways comprise an internal market, with reciprocal adjustments by both the business and the Provider organization.

2.7.2. Purpose

Maturity models are invaluable management tools. They can be applied to individuals, e.g. child to adolescent to adult; applied to organizations, e.g. start-up to growth to mature; and even to entire ecosystems, e.g. diffusion of innovation. Richard Nolan was among the first to propose a maturity model for IT management with his Stage Theory in the 1970s.

The Software Engineering Institute at Carnegie Mellon University contributed much to contemporary best practice in IT process improvement with a capability maturity approach known as Capability Maturity Model Integration (CMMI). Typically used in an *inside out* approach for assessing capability maturity and determining improvement practices, CMMI takes a firm position that process management is the key to IT improvement.

By contrast, the Business-Provider Maturity Model is used both as a diagnostic—to surface the maturity of business demand for Provider services and capabilities and of Provider supply capabilities—and as a *dialogic* to drive dialog about business demand and Provider supply maturity and how these are evolving. The model can be used for an enterprise as a whole or for a given business unit or Provider capability unit.

2.7.3. Characteristics of the Business-Provider Maturity Model

In its simplest form, the model is an S-shaped learning curve—the business learning to exploit technology (or whatever services and/or products the Provider supplies) and the Provider organization learning to become efficient and effective in delivering services and, especially as maturity increases, shaping business demand. Business executives often find the model's simple elegance appealing. They quickly grasp the concepts behind business demand maturity and are able to use the model to analyze how their demand maturity is evolving over time. This equips them to engage in meaningful dialogue with Provider leadership about the business implications of both demand and supply maturity.

Figure 10 depicts the basic 3-level model. Note that the number of levels is arbitrary. It sometimes makes sense to use a 5-level model, which can be useful with its finer-grained approach, but the simplicity of the 3-level model works well for most purposes and avoids *false precision.*

2.7.4. Business-Provider Maturity Model

To the left of the S-curve are the characteristics of business demand at each of 3 levels. To the right are the corresponding goals of Provider supply (in this case, IT). It is important to recognize this is a developmental model. As such, it is cumulative—the demand at lower levels never goes away—the business always wants *the lights kept on,* (a Level 1 demand). An IT organization that fails to supply against this demand will lack credibility and wherewithal to move up the maturity curve. As business demand matures to Level 2, for example, Level 1 demand for efficiency does not go away—it becomes a fundamental expectation—*table stakes.*

Level 1 business demand is typically generated from functional and geographic silos—often much to the frustration of IT leaders, who are able to look across the enterprise and see many opportunities for cross-functional processes and collaboration, but are unable to *sell* such concepts. Level 1 demand is primarily for foundational transaction processing solutions and operational data—all with an overarching goal of reducing the costs of doing business. Level 1 supply, in addition to satisfying business demand, focuses on the basic *blocking and tackling* of IT management—for example, project management and stable IT operations.

Level 2 demand (which is additive to Level 1 demand) tackles enterprise integration and consolidated management information. Level 2 supply is focused on deploying a common infrastructure and enterprise systems implementation. Level 2 supply also focuses on *IT as a business* with attention to portfolio management, service management and getting faster at delivering solutions.

Level 3 demand (which is additive to Level 2 and 3 demand) typically addresses IT-enabled business growth and innovation. It tends to be much more externally focused than Level 1 and 2, interested in business intelligence, rapid experimentation and collaboration—both with other business units and with customers and suppliers.

Note: Business demand and Provider supply are interdependent. A low maturity supply organization tends to limit business demand—stifles the appetite, as it were, whereas high supply maturity tends to stimulate demand—introducing innovative ideas and opportunities, for example. Similarly, high business demand tends to drive high supply maturity, while low business demand suppresses supply maturity. As such, business demand maturity and Provider supply maturity are rarely more than one-half step or so out of synchronization. If the gap between supply and demand widens beyond one-half step, there is usually a major intervention, such as replacing the head of the Provider organization (for either over-building or under-building supply capabilities) or wholesale outsourcing of Provider capabilities.

2.7.5. Characteristics of Level 1 Business-Provider Maturity

Note: In the descriptions of the characteristics below, we use IT as the Provider organization as the example. Please customize this to your specific Provider domain if it is other than IT.

At Level 1, business demand is focused on efficiency. Level 1 demand typically originates independently in various business units and functions, operating as *silos*. Demand at this level is primarily about transaction automation (e.g. replacing clerical activity with information systems) in pursuit of cost savings. The information appetite is for operational data—What did we produce or accomplish? How does that stack up against goals and past performance? Given that Level 1 demand tends to originate within business silos, the orientation and focus is generally limited to those silos (e.g. sales, service, production, finance, and human resources) and often bounded by specific geographies (e.g. sales within a given country or region).

IT supply at Level 1 focuses on basic transaction processing (e.g. order fulfillment, claims processing, and payroll) and basic IT services (e.g., desktop computing and help desk) plus any custom solutions or modifications to packaged software demanded by the business. The communications networks are typically *closed*—limited to the corporation and specific connections with suppliers and customers. Because information systems are built and managed for functional silos, a lot of work goes into application and database interfaces that help connect *islands of automation* and make useful operational information available. Most IT work is performed in-house, with the help of a few key hardware, software, and services vendors.

At Level 1, the Provider's goal is to improve the infrastructure in order to provide stable, reliable operations and business support—sometimes unglamorously referred to as *keeping the lights on.*

2.7.6. Characteristics of Level 2 Business-Provider Maturity

At Level 2, business demand evolves from a focus on business efficiency to effectiveness. It typically becomes more cross-functional than the siloed demand common to Level 1, since achieving business effectiveness often requires functional silos to work together with end-to-end processes (e.g. order to cash). So Level 2 demand has more to do with business integration than simple functional performance. And integration extends beyond corporate boundaries, relying on information exchange and closer operating coordination with selected customers and suppliers. As such, the information appetite at Level 2 shifts from simply transactional data to management information—Who are our most profitable customers? Who are our most critical suppliers?

IT supply at Level 2 focuses on enterprise systems, such as ERP and CRM. At this level, services to enable and support the effective use of enterprise systems become important—capabilities such as Data Warehousing and Business Analytics. Communications networks tend to open up, with specific gateways to the Internet and more general inter-enterprise connections for electronic commerce. A key activity at Level 2 is building common infrastructure (hardware, software, databases and data warehouses, information management tools) thereby reducing redundancy, reliance on custom interfaces, and lowering IT cost. IT sourcing shifts to a more flexible and integrated approach, with a limited set of *strategic* partners. Often, Level 2 sees *commodity* IT services being outsourced. IT's automation goals shift from basic transaction processes to business process improvement and re-engineering. That means IT competencies shift in balance from technical to business process orientation, with business analysis and relationship management as important disciplines.

At Level 2, the Provider's goal is to improve solution delivery in order to become more efficient, effective and agile in meeting business needs for solutions.

2.7.7. Characteristics of Level 3 Business-Provider Maturity

At Level 3, business demand shifts in focus from effectiveness to innovation and growth. The appetite for information expands to include business and market intelligence, based on more extensive data and sophisticated analytics—What *share of wallet* do we command among our most profitable customers? What customer segments offer the greatest potential for greater share? The business appetite for IT (though rarely articulated in these terms) is to enable agility. In order to connect with a fast-changing ecosystem, to innovate quickly and seize opportunities, a business must have all of its critical assets (talent, processes, technology, and trading relationships) structured and managed as an easily reconfigurable portfolio of capabilities. That's the architecture of business agility—one that IT has a crucial role in enabling.

At Level 3, IT supply is focused on strategic and technology-driven business capabilities—putting information and technology to use at the heart of the company's value proposition and leveraging technology as the catalyst for marketplace differentiation. Communications networks are largely *open* in order to flexibly connect with the larger ecosystem. The corporate infrastructure evolves to be a more agile platform, with standard interfaces and capabilities opened to Business Partners. IT services and capabilities are sourced wherever the best price/ performance may be, sometimes halfway around the globe. Again, the emphasis is on flexibility (e.g. Software as a Service, Platform as a Service, Infrastructure as a Service) to facilitate rapid creation, scaling, and dissolution of services.

At Level 3, the Provider's goal is help the business innovate and grow.

2.7.8. Using the Business-Provider Maturity Model

At its heart, the model is a communications and calibration tool. For this reason, it is deliberately simple and evocative. Any business executive can engage in a meaningful discussion of business demand and IT supply and how these change over time. To use the model systematically, you might use it to assess and drive discussion of:

- The current state of business demand and Provider supply and how well they are aligned.
- Gaps between supply and demand, their significance, and how best to close them.
- How business demand maturity might vary by business unit, and how to accommodate and even leverage unevenness in business demand.
- The Provider Operating Model and how this should evolve to drive changes in Business-Provider maturity.

The model is intentionally simple to grasp and relatively open-ended. The model is a management tool, not a scientific instrument. Its primary purpose and value lie in driving dialogue, especially among business and Provider leaders, about the current state and potential evolution of business demand and Provider supply. In the process, they can align priorities, resources, and ambitions; clarifying strategic intents for the business use of technology; stimulate business appetite for Provider capabilities; and maximize the current and future business value of those services and assets.

One of the keys in using the model is scope, or *unit of analysis*. There can be value in assessing average demand and supply maturity across an enterprise. However, while averages can be useful, they can also be misleading. It may be more enlightening to apply the model to a business unit, division, or segment, especially if demand and/ or supply maturity vary substantially across units. Knowing, for example, that business demand in Business Unit A is low Level 3, while in Business Units B and C it is high Level 1, could have significant implications for appointing business-IT relationship managers and designing shared IT services across the three units.

2.7.9. Moving to the Business-Provider Maturity Next Level

Moving to the next level in Business-Provider Maturity always involves discontinuity. You can't reach Level 2 by simply getting better and better at Level 1 activities. To reach Level 2, both the business and IT organizations have to do new things, unlearn some old ways, and do old things in different ways.

Moving from one level to the next typically involves new methods and techniques. More challenging, it involves breakthroughs in mindset, ambitions, and values. When the business and IT reach equilibrium at one level, ITs customers may express everyday satisfaction, but the perceived business value of IT will gradually decline. After all, IT is doing the *same old stuff*, albeit well. If business and IT leadership are alert to the business potential of technology, then pressure builds to increase the business value of IT investments, assets, and initiatives—and the move to the next level.

Level 3 creates business possibilities that don't exist at lower levels. Yes, you can achieve isolated business product and process innovation at all levels, but typically it's through heroics—and heroics are neither sustainable

nor widespread. At Level 3, powerful, agile IT capabilities exist across the company, reinforced by leadership vision, collaboration and excellence in management processes and disciplines.

We refer to the challenges common to the transition from low-to-mid Level 2 Business-IT Maturity to Level 3 as Sticking Points.

2.8. Business Relationship Maturity Model

The Business Relationship Maturity Model (BRMM) is a way to help surface and understand the maturity of the relationship between a Provider (e.g. internal IT organization) and their Business Partner.

Note: The BRMM is about the maturity of the Provider/Business Partner relationship, not of the BRM role.

Overview of the Business Relationship Maturity Model

The Business Relationship Maturity Model (BRMM) depicts a 5-level relationship maturity continuum, where the uppermost (5th) level is a notional ideal state where the Business-Provider relationship fulfills the aspirations of both the Provider and its Business Partner. At this level, the relationship would be systematically managed and continuously improved. The BRMM has been developed to help assess the strength of their Business Partner-Provider relationships and take appropriate actions to improve those relationships and the value realized from investments the Business Partner makes in the Provider's services and capabilities.

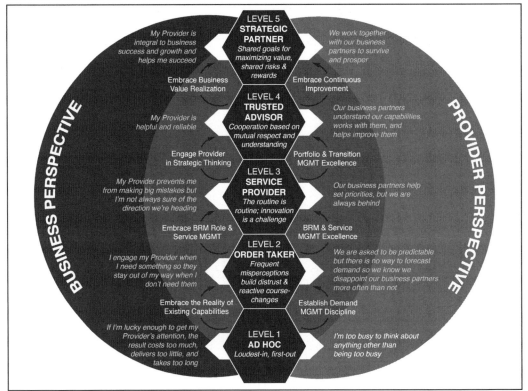

Figure 11 - Business Relationship Maturity Model

2.8.1. Overview of Business Relationship Maturity

The BRMM speaks to 5 Levels of Relationship Maturity. Figure 11 describes each level in summary through a short list of Characteristics. Each level is further characterized from both a business perspective—the business view of the Provider, and from a Provider perspective—the Provider view of the business. Each perspective at each level is described through the four BRM Core Disciplines. Finally, the model suggests strategies for both the Provider and the Business to be undertaken to get to the next level.

2.8.2. Using the Business Relationship Maturity Model

Here are several ways to use the Business Relationship Maturity Model:

- To assess the current Business Relationship Maturity in your enterprise, to help clarify the overall context in which you need to approach BRM implementation (i.e. where to begin with BRM)

- To set targets for Business Relationship Maturity over a time horizon (e.g. which Maturity Level do we want to reach by when) and construct a plan for reaching those targets (using the *Getting to Level X* parts of the model)

- To educate your BRM team and Provider leaders on the current state of Business Relationship Maturity at your enterprise, where you are headed, and how they key stakeholders should participate in elevating Business Relationship Maturity

- As food for thought as you prepare for discussions with your Business Partners or in using the Relationship Strategy on a Page Strategic Partnering technique

- As information for you as you approach various Business Relationship Management activities, as the maturity level may shape your approach (e.g. discovery, demand shaping/management, capability roadmapping, portfolio management, etc.)

2.9. Business-Provider Alignment

The Business-Provider Alignment Model helps to understand and analyze the four key elements of alignment—business environment, strategic context, Provider strategy, and Provider investment portfolio. It illustrates the *barriers* that typically surround these elements and impede alignment.

2.9.1. Background

The Business-Provider Alignment model is a generalized version of the Business-IT Alignment framework published in the groundbreaking book, *Leveraging the New Infrastructure: How Market Leaders Capitalize on IT* by Peter Weill and Marianne Broadbent, published in 1998. In many respects, the concept of Business-IT Alignment is anachronistic in today's age where just about everything is digitized and technology is becoming increasingly consumerized. Some talk about the convergence of business and IT as a more appropriate way of maximizing the strategic value of IT. Nevertheless, the alignment framework in Figure 12 can help surface constructive dialog about the relationship between Provider investments, the business they support and the barriers that inhibit alignment, let alone convergence.

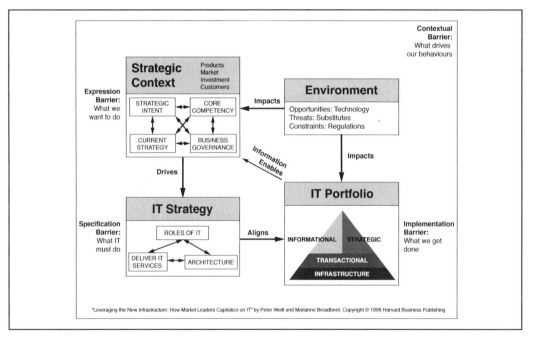

Figure 12 - Business-Provider Alignment Model – Barriers to Alignment

2.9.2. Purpose

The alignment model in Figure 12 can be used to surface dialog about the relationship between Provider investments and the business they support. It can be particularly helpful in understanding the common barriers to alignment, such as the Contextual Barrier that drives business and Provider behaviors, the Expression barriers that obscure business strategy, the Specification barriers that obscure Provider strategy, the Implementation barriers that obscure the Provider portfolio and its value as a strategic alignment tool.

2.9.3. The Alignment Model

The model illustrates four elements:

1. The Environment within which the business operates.
2. The Strategic Context for the business.
3. The Provider Strategy.
4. The Provider Portfolio of investments, assets and capabilities.

Of note are the relationships among these elements. The Environment impacts the Strategic Context. The Strategic Context both drives the Provider Strategy and is enabled by the Provider Investment Portfolio. In other words, a weak set of Provider assets and capabilities, or a poorly managed set of Provider investments limits strategic options.

2.9.4. The Expression Barrier

The Strategic Context can be hard to nail down in any specific terms. There is usually some form of articulated business strategy, but sometimes it is vague and unclear as to what is actually meant by the strategy. "Grow international sales" and "Increase share of wallet" are noble goals, but tell you little to nothing about what must be accomplished to achieve them. Often there is a disconnect between articulated strategy (Strategic Intent) and the actual strategy in action. Talking to the most senior executives will often give you a reasonable sense of Strategic Intent, but talking to line business managers reflects something quite different—often driven by performance management systems and prior strategies that have supposedly been replaced!

Weill and Broadbent refer to these disconnects and holes in Business Strategy as an Expression Barrier.

2.9.5. The Specification Barrier

If the business strategic context can be baffling due to the Expression Barrier that surrounds it, the Provider strategy can be equally unclear due to the Specification Barrier. Getting clear on the Role of the Provider in the enterprise can be challenging. For example, is it an enabler or a strategic driver? Should it respond to business strategy or inform it? Reaching consensus on this across key stakeholders can be very difficult.

Once the Provider role is clarified, figuring out what Provider capabilities are needed, and how they should be best sourced can be equally challenging—especially as global sourcing options continually expand and shift.

Finally, governing the Provider as a strategic business capability is a constant challenge for most companies. Getting business executives to understand and agree to the necessary priorities for IT investments demanded by the business strategy is difficult—they would sooner simply pass the demand *over the wall* and let the Provider organization figure out how to meet that demand.

2.9.6. The Implementation Barrier

Finally, there are many things that conspire to form a barrier to implementing a portfolio that properly enables the business Strategic Context and aligns with the Provider strategy. For example, poorly integrated Provider infrastructure (the common base of Provider services that enable the enterprise) following years of acquisitions and mergers that were *left alone* drive up the cost of that infrastructure, restrict its flexibility, and starve investments from Utility transaction processing, investment in IT capabilities that Enhance business capability, and investment in new Frontier capabilities that could drive growth and business innovation.

2.9.7. The Contextual Barrier

The Cultural Context is deeply ingrained and can include such factors as the culture of accountability, clarity of roles and rules of engagement, the degree to which an organization is *relationship driven* versus *rules and roles driven*, the organizations resilience to change, and so on.

2.10. Business Partner's Decision Cycle

The Business Partner's Decision Cycle is a useful way to understand, assess and improve the nature of the Business Partner-Provider relationship.

2.10.1. Background

Figure 13 represents a simplified decision process that Business Partners go through when thinking about strategy and how a Providers services and capabilities can enable that strategy. It comprises 6 steps—from identifying strategic possibilities to selecting solutions.

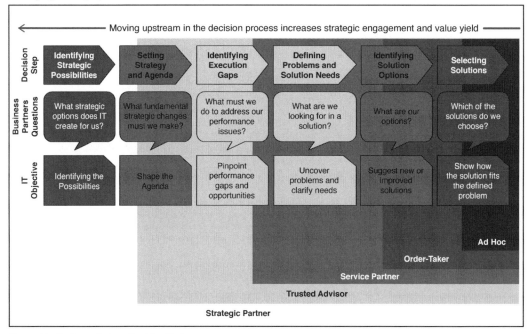

Figure 13 - Business Partner Decision Cycle

2.10.2. Purpose

Helping to surface the Business Partner's decision process—one that is usually subconscious and implicit—to help the BRM to engage as early in the process as possible. Ideally, the BRM should engage with their Business Partner in the initial step—when identifying strategic possibilities. This affords the strongest opportunity for shaping business demand towards the highest value opportunities.

Business Relationship Maturity Levels

1. *Ad Hoc*—demand is essentially unmanaged; rules of engagement between Business Partner and Provider are unclear and inconsistent; there is a lack of Service Management discipline; there is no clear sense of Provider service cost or value.

2. *Order Taker*—demand is prioritized based upon weak or subjective data; frequent misperceptions build distrust; the Provider is reactive and does not challenge business requests; there is a lack of quality data to support cost or value analyses.

3. *Service Partner*—there is a clear process for engagement—at least for steady state services; steady state services are consistent, but major projects and programs are inconsistent and not fully predictable; costs are transparent, but value is subjective.

4. *Trusted Adviser*—there is a mutual understanding and appreciation of capabilities and needs; the Provider service portfolio is appropriate to business needs; the Provider engages early and often in Business Partner decision cycle, and an increasing sense of value from investments in Provider services and capabilities.

5. *Strategic Partner*—Provider and Business Partner share common goals with a focus on business value realization; there is clear accountability for achieving value from investments in Provider services and capabilities and quality data to support value analyses.

2.10.3. Ad Hoc Relationship

An Ad Hoc Business Partner-Provider relationship engages when the Business Partner is selecting solutions, and in some cases, after the solution has already been selected by the Business Partner! It is virtually impossible for the Provider to add value at that stage.

2.10.4. Order-Taker Relationship

A slightly better point of engagement is when the Business Partner is identifying solution options. In this type of relationship, the Business Partner is typically asking: "What are our solution options?" and the Provider is suggesting new or improved solutions. Success occurs when the solution has been defined and accepted by the Business Partner.

The Order-Taker Relationship is often the default when no specific or focused actions have been taken to formalize the BRM role. Figure 14 illustrates such a case of the Business Partner experience.

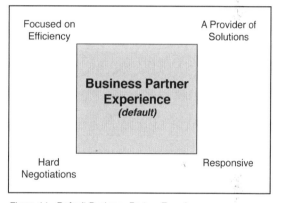

Figure 14 - Default Business Partner Experience

2.10.5. Service Partner Relationship

At this point in the decision cycle, the Business Partner is looking to the Provider to help define business problems and potential solutions, and may even ask for help examining execution gaps—gaps in business capability that prevent business strategy being realized.

2.10.6. Trusted Advisor Relationship

In a Trusted Advisor relationship, the Business Partner involves the Provider in activities such as clarifying business strategy, for example, working with the BRM to create a Business Capability Roadmap for strategy deployment.

2.10.7. Strategic Partner Relationship

The most valuable form of Business Partner-Provider relationship is when the Provider is helping formulate business strategy, in addition to creating the Business Capability Roadmap that deploys that strategy.

Page Intentionally Left Blank

3. Organizing BRM

As an organizational role, the Business Relationship Manager is a connector, orchestrator, and navigator between a Provider organization and one or more business units.

Most BRMs have the role as a full time position, whereas CIOs and heads of Provider organizations fill the BRM role for the enterprise as a part time role.

3.1. Typical BRM Activities Across the Provider Capability Model

Another way to define and communicate the BRM role is to consider how that role plays into each top-level Capability in the Provider Capability Model. Figure 15 illustrates how the BRM role contributes to each Capability, and that Business Relationship Management is much more than simply managing relationships.

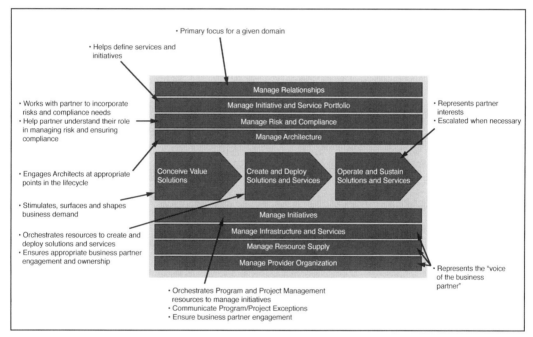

Figure 15 - Typical BRM Activities Across the Provider Capability Model

3.2. Strategic versus Tactical BRM

Comparison of the Strategic and Tactical BRM role variations. The former operates in the context of business strategy and Provider initiatives intended to enact business strategy. The latter tends to operate in the context of Service Management and is primarily concerned with steady state services.

3.2.1. Strategic BRM

The strategic BRM is usually a senior member of the Provider organization—often a Director or Vice President level executive—interfacing with business unit heads and senior executives. Their focus is value realization and tends to emphasize initiatives (projects, programs, investments) intended to enact business strategy.

3.2.2. Tactical BRM

The tactical BRM is usually a senior business analyst, qualified in Service Management and interfacing with mid-level business unit managers and staff. They are mostly concerned with Service Management. Excellence in Service Management (and therefore the importance of the tactical BRM role) is crucial for the Strategic BRM role to gain traction. As it is said, "It is hard for the strategic BRM to gain a seat at the business strategy table when the lights don't stay on or the trains don't run on time!" The tactical BRM, as a key Service Management resource, helps ensure that "the lights stay on and the trains run on time!"

3.2.3. Importance of BRM Role Clarity

The strategic and tactical BRM roles are easily confused, but this confusion should be avoided. Once a BRM has established through their behaviors that they are tactical, that is the way they will be seen by Business Partners and they may have a hard time moving to a more strategic BRM role. Their Business Partners will tend to see them as a technical rather than a strategic resource. So, it is important to position the BRM clearly with both their Business Partners and within the Provider organization.

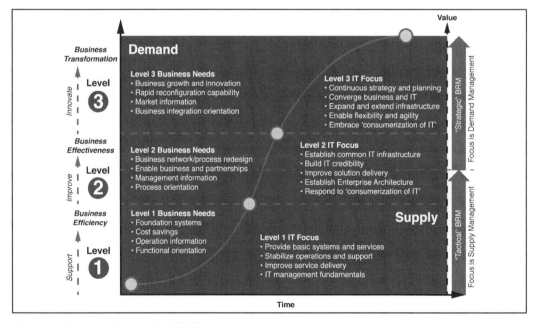

Figure 16 - The Maturity Model and the BRM Role

3.3. Common BRM Reporting and Organization Structures

Some examples of common BRM role reporting and organization structures.

3.3.1. Background

We see many types of BRM reporting relationships, including:

- Solid line to Provider lead, dotted line to Business Partner lead
- Dotted line to Provider lead, solid line to Business Partner lead
- Some BRMs report to Provider Strategy and/or Architecture lead, PMO, etc.

We see many variations in BRM staff, from:

- No staff (BRM as individual performer)
- Multi-level BRM groups:
- BRM Lead
- BRM Manager
- BRM Analyst
- Small supply team (e.g. mini-CIO organization, *shadow* Provider organization)

3.3.2. BRM-Business Partner Alignment

The earliest BRM model was as a bridge between a business unit (e.g. sales, manufacturing) and an IT organization. As businesses have become more process-centric, it is common to see a BRM bridging between an end-to-end business process (e.g. procure-to-pay) and a Provider (e.g. IT). Some BRMs operate at an Enterprise level. The Enterprise BRM role is often an implied role for the Provider head (e.g. CIO or VP HR).

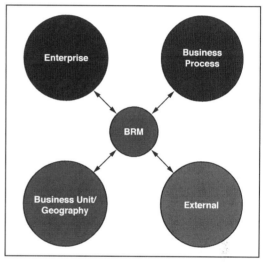

Figure 17 - Business Relationship Manager Alignment

3.4. Demand Shaping

Demand Shaping (sometimes referred to as *Demand Management*) is the process by which possibilities for using the Provider's services within the business are surfaced and capitalized upon. The goal is to identify that set of possibilities that will create the most value for the organization.

For the purposes of understanding the BRM role and discipline, it is useful to think of Demand Shaping as a set of competencies, tools, and governance mechanisms designed to surface, stimulate and shape business demand for Provider products and services in balance with supply constraints.

3.4.1. Background

Delivering Provider products and services, especially when the Provider is an IT organization, has been challenging since businesses first became IT-dependent. There's lots of complexity, layers of specialization, an unnatural separation of IT producer and consumer, and significant capital investments. Exacerbating this is the typically high ongoing maintenance and life cycle costs, rapidly changing generations of technology, with resulting technological obsolescence. As a result, IT leaders have focused far more on supply management—figuring out their supply chains, providing security, integrity and stable services, squeezing out costs,and so on.

Meanwhile, the demand side has typically received short shrift. Demand chains are unclear at best, and complexities such as the IT infrastructure implications of supply activities and changing technologies are opaque. IT planners have a hard time answering fundamental questions such as, "What's in the pipeline for the next 6 months?" or, "What is our projected resource utilization for the next 6 months?"

There are also common problems where demand meets supply—IT delivers products and services that business users don't understand, did not really want, or did want but do not know how to extract the business value. It is generally seen that IT's job is to "deliver" the solution, but not to ensure it is working to full effect.

3.4.2. Purpose

According to Wikipedia:

> *Demand management is a planning methodology used to manage and forecast the demand of products and services. In business, the term is used to describe the **proactive management of work initiatives (demand) with business constraints (supply)**. (bold font added for emphasis)*

For the purposes of understanding the BRM role, we define Demand Shaping as:

> *A set of disciplines, tools, and governance mechanisms designed to surface, stimulate and shape business demand for IT products and services in balance with supply constraints.*

In other words, given that IT supply is always limited, how do we surface and shape demand to get optimum business value from limited IT supply?

Note: we use the term *Demand Shaping* rather than *Demand Management* which for some people and organizations may have negative connotations.

3.4.3. Key Elements of Demand Shaping

Getting Demand Shaping working effectively requires an orchestration of several techniques and processes—and ultimately, a moderate to high level of Business-IT Maturity (earned through the focus on supply management mentioned above).

The key elements include:

- Portfolio Management is an important demand management technique and tool (and, if implemented properly, a governance mechanism). Portfolio Management can help balance IT demand across time horizons (short versus long term), across risk/reward profiles (high-risk/high potential return, low-risk/low potential return), across business units or business processes, and across IT investment categories, such as IT projects and programs versus IT infrastructure. Portfolio Management can make these balancing acts explicit so that they become strategic choices (Portfolio Planning) rather than the result of natural "drift."

- Product Management and Service Life Cycle Management. In the world of IT, creating a solution is a fraction of the cost—maintaining and evolving it, keeping up with changing business needs and shifting technologies is costly. Traditional accounting practices add to the load as depreciation of capital expenditures creates an ongoing drag on funding sources. So, ensuring that life cycle costs are taken into account with the initial investment, and managing product life cycles to ensure that necessary investments are made, and unnecessary products and services are retired in a timely fashion is a key Product and Service Management function. Also, maximizing *reuse* of products and services—"why bring in yet another Customer Relationship Management system when we already have three" is a common refrain that often goes unanswered. Finally, understanding cost drivers, and influencing business behavior towards *responsible consumption* of IT products and services is an important part of the demand management equation.

- Business Relationship Management (BRM)—the key interface between business and IT. The BRM is an important demand management channel. Effective demand management hinges on highly skilled Business Relationship Mangers who posses a strong business understanding and trusting relationships.

- Project Management is mostly a supply management technique. However, poor project management can negatively impact demand. For example, we see business behavior that essentially says, "I will ask for more than I need because I know IT will screw it up!" Or, "I will ask for as much as I can get because I know nobody is keeping count on the results!"

- Program Management embodies an important set of both Demand and Supply Management disciplines, tools and governance mechanisms. Program Management is a critical linkage between Portfolio Management and Project Management.

- Agile Supply Capabilities, including the ability to rapidly prototype, or to conduct business experiments to validate or clarify a need is important to demand management. This is one of the best reasons for techniques such as selective outsourcing and cloud computing—being able to flex up as demand increases and scale back when it wanes.

- Robust Business-Provider Governance. In particular, governance must address how demand is justified, funded, and how benefits are tracked and accountability held for them.

3.5. The BRM Role in Practice

3.5.1. Background

Approaches to defining and implementing the BRM role and organizational capabilities vary widely in practice across many dimensions, including:

- Strategic vs. Tactical BRM—some BRM roles are defined and staffed as senior positions (e.g. Vice President, Director) facing off with senior business executives and focused on strategic issues (e.g. helping the business define their strategy as enabled by the Providers products, services and capabilities. Others define the BRM role as a relatively junior position (e.g. Business Analyst) focused on more tactical (but nonetheless extremely important) issues such as service level definition and the service catalog.
- Seniority—and level of business executive with whom the BRM partners.
- Purpose—especially in the balance of focus between supply (the view from the Provider out to the Business Partner) and demand (the view from the Business Partner back to the Provider).
- Title—e.g. Business Partner Director, Account Manager, etc.
- Supply side focus—e.g. IT, HR, Finance, Line of Business, etc.
- Demand side focus—e.g. Line of Business, Business Process, Geography.
- Team size—from sole practitioner to leader of a team of 10+.
- Numbers of BRMs per enterprise—from 1 to 100s.
- Career trajectory—often moving from major project or program management role to leadership role in Provider domain (e.g. to CIO).

3.5.2. Typical Scope

Scope that is Common to both Strategic and Tactical BRM Models

- Shapes and monitors services, service levels and service performance
- Partners with Provider to manage expectations, ensure service delivery and improve service performance
- Ensures Business Partner awareness of security requirements / policies / responsibilities
- Orchestrates key Provider roles on behalf of Business Partner
- Reinforces Service Management discipline and competence

Scope that is Unique to Strategic BRM

- Strategic interface between Business Partner and Provider organization
- Ensures strategic alignment between business strategy and Provider capabilities
- Jointly accountable for business case and portfolio
- Ensures value is realized from Provider capabilities, assets and investments
- Surfaces and shapes business demand for Provider services
- Coordinates with other BRMs to identify, align, and leverage enterprise opportunities
- Acts as a broker for additional capabilities beyond Provider scope

3.5.3. Typical BRM Decision Rights

Role	Multi-year Strategy	Ideation	Analysis	Design	Testing	Maintenance & Operations	Value Optimization
BRM	R	A	A	C	C	I	R
Business Partner	A	R	R	C	R	C	A
Enterprise Architecture	R	C	R	C	I	C	C
Solution Delivery	I	C	R	A	R	C	I
PMO	I	I	R	R	R	I	I
Infrastructure / Operations	I	I	I	I	A	A	I

Responsible - "The doer"

Accountable - "The buck stops here"

Consulted - "In the loop"

Informed - "Keep in the picture"

Figure 18 - Typical BRM Decisions Rights

3.5.4. Types of Relationship Management Role

Technical Expert

Pros	Cons
Experts like it, equate it with high status	Can detract from professional credibility
Some Business Partners may sometimes demand it	Fosters dependence, creates parent-child dynamics
	Vulnerable to abuse

Technical Experts may be recognized for their expertise, but still not be credible as BRMs.

From Expertise to Credibility

Credibility requires both expertise and trustworthiness. We tend to trust people:

- Who have similar background or worldviews to ourselves.
- With whom we've experienced positive interactions over time.
- Who present themselves and behave appropriately in our eyes.
- Who are consistent in their behaviors – especially in doing what they said they will do.

Chapter 3

Earning Trust

Trust can be earned, but not simply by being a technical expert! We view as experts those we trust, but we don't necessarily trust experts! Trust is built up over time through the skills of relationship management—in particular, by:

- Active listening
- Creating positive interactions with Business Partners
- Helping Business Partners become self-sufficient
- Teaching and coaching
- Responding well in difficult Business Partner encounters
- Avoiding defensiveness
- By building multiyear strategies and corresponding capability roadmaps and delivering or showing results against that roadmap

The Technical Expert is really a distortion of the BRM role—you may need technical experts supporting your Business Partners, but calling them BRMs limits the value of the role. Many BRMs have a technical background, which is fine. However, there is a potential trap—when the Business Partner asks you to solve a technical issue, and you do so, you will forever more be seen as a Technical Expert, and may have disqualified yourself for a more strategic engagement with that Business Partner. It's easy to fall into the Technical Expert trap—but it's hard to climb back out!

3.5.5. Service Provider

The Service Provider role tends to be a step up in perceived value from the Technical Expert towards the Business Partnership role.

Pros	Cons
Consistent with managers' line role expectations	The "Customer is not always right"—serving their needs may not be in the organization's best interests
Business Partners often prefer it to the Technical Expert role	Creates conflicts of interest of who is in charge and competing priorities.
May be a necessary step toward partnership	Fosters *order taking* which is not valued, often leads to the BRM being treated as menials and being blamed when orders are wrong

3.5.6. Business Partner

The Business Partner Relationship Role has the highest potential to create value for the Business Partner.

Pros	Cons
It has the highest potential to create value for the Business Partner	With shared rewards come shared risks
It provides an opportunity to share rewards with the Business Partner	Sometimes, the role demands confrontation with the Business Partner (e.g. pushing back on low-value demand in order to stimulate higher value opportunities)
It provides an opportunity to be "part of the team" with the Business Partner	Not every opportunity is appropriate for a strategic partnership—some activities are transactional or service provisioning

The notion of "partnership" gets a lot of lip-service, but the reality is that it takes at least two to form a partnership—I can't be your partner unless you are willing to be my partner. BRMs operate in a partnership role by adding value through seeing opportunities that Business Partners don't see or want to see and selling the Business Partner on those opportunities. Successful BRMs know when to cajole, when to confront, and when to give in—in short, by political behavior.

Page Intentionally Left Blank

4.   Service Provisioning

Providing Services to the business requires an understanding of enterprise governance of IT, Service Management, and Portfolio Management. This chapter addresses these topics from a BRM perspective.

4.1.   Business-IT Governance

Business-IT Governance describes the framework of decision rights and accountabilities and the structures and policies that support the framework to encourage desired behavior to realize maximum value from information technology. It formalizes how business makes decisions about the deployment and delivery of IT throughout the enterprise.

4.1.1. Background

Effective Business-IT Governance aligns IT decision-making with Enterprise governance and business unit objectives through an interrelated set of processes, policies and decision-making structures with clear goals, roles and functions, sponsored by the CEO, with clear consequences for compliance or lack thereof.

4.1.2. Purpose

Business-IT Governance strives to achieve a proper balance between:

- Variety vs. Stability
- Innovation vs. Standardization
- Autonomy vs. Collaboration

It manages IT investments and assets as a shared resource and provides a "strategy transmission chain" from senior executives on down through the organization.

When sound IT Governance is in place, senior executives not only know their organization's IT plans and policies, they also know how they are made.

4.1.3. Separating Governance from Management

According to COBIT 5:

> Governance ensures that stakeholders needs, conditions and options are evaluated to determine balanced, agreed-on enterprise objectives to be achieved; setting direction through prioritization and decision making; and monitoring performance and compliance against agreed-on direction and objectives.

Management plans, builds, runs, and monitors activities in alignment with the direction set by the governance body to achieve enterprise objectives.

Objectives

- Decisions regarding IT are made at the right level
- Issues of enterprise strategy and business operating model are business decisions
- Demand is managed based on business value
- Supply is managed by the Provider Leadership Team

Recipes for failure

- Focusing too narrowly on approval of new initiatives (which ignores 70%-90% of spending)

- Fails to revisit/terminate initiatives
- Failing to consult constituencies before a decision is made
- Not adequately communicating decisions and the decision making process
- Not working with constituencies to translate decisions into new behaviors
- Not integrating IT governance into business governance, especially capital allocation and funding

4.1.4. Decision Rights and Accountabilities

Characteristics

Clarify who is responsible (R), accountable (A), is consulted (C), and is informed (I) on decisions (RACI charting)

Issues

- Most infrastructure decisions tend to be Provider driven with insufficient business understanding
- Senior Management perceives low value from Provider investments (especially IT)
- Mechanisms to make Provider decisions are slow or contradictory and often reside at the top of the Provider hierarchy (unclear decision rights create a slow decision process)

4.1.5. Best Practices

- Provide clarity of decision rights at a RACI level to all Provider and business stakeholders
- Use RACI across all the Provider Domains
- Involve Senior business managers in decision rights for appropriate domains

4.2. Key Business-IT Governance Domains

4.2.1. Business-IT Principles

High level statements about how IT is used in the firm—capture the essence of the firm's future direction and how IT will be used to get there.

4.2.2. Enterprise Architecture

Synchronizes IT and business strategy by focusing on the IT components that enable critical business processes—the organizing logic for business processes, information, data, applications, and infrastructure is captured in a set of policies and technical choices, intended to enable the firm's business strategy.

4.2.3. IT Infrastructure Strategies

Describe the approach for building the IT foundation for the firm—made up of the shared and standard IT services include requirements for infrastructure capability as well as the location of capabilities within the firm.

4.2.4. Business Application Needs

Specify the business need for purchased or internally developed IT applications.

4.2.5. IT Investments, Prioritization and Value Realization

Decisions about how much and where to invest in IT business solutions including project approvals and justification techniques—covers the whole IT investment decision-making and accountability process.

4.3. Business-IT Governance Illustration

Enterprise

Enterprise IT Board

CIO
IT Leadership Team

PMO

Portfolio & Program
Management Office

Enterprise Architecture Council

**Business Unit
or Business Process**

Business Unit/Process IT Boards

BRM + Business Unit - Aligned IT

Key: ▪ Governance Structure ▪ Organization Structure

Figure 19 - Business IT Governance Example

Enterprise Level Business-IT Governance

The highest level is an Enterprise IT Board, which would typically comprise the CEO, CIO and Business Unit heads. The Chair would be any of these individuals, except the CIO, and would rotate periodically.

As a linking mechanism, the CIO also leads the IT Leadership Team, which, in addition to its functional management responsibilities, acts collectively as a governance body—usually focused on IT Infrastructure and internal departmental investment decisions.

The PMO (Portfolio and Program Management Office) typically reports to the CIO and is a key mechanism to support Business-IT Governance.

An Enterprise Architecture Council is the senior architectural governance body and is usually chaired by the lead Enterprise Architect, who is a member of the IT Leadership Team, so there is linkage between that team and Enterprise Architecture governance.

Business Unit or Business Process Business-IT Governance

Below the Enterprise Level (issues that cut across all business units and processes) is Business-IT Governance for Business Units and/or end-to-end Business Processes (e.g. Supply Chain, Order-to-Cash). This level is usually comprised of Business Unit and/or Business Process IT Boards.

There are sometimes Business Unit and/or Business Process aligned IT organizations led by BRMs. These work closely with their respective Business Unit and/or Business Process IT Boards.

4.4. Service Management

Service Management embodies a number of disciplines used to optimize service-intensive supply chains. These disciplines include Strategic Service Management, Service Strategy and Customer Management. One special application is IT Service Management which includes the International Standard ISO/IEC 20000 and the ITIL® Framework.

4.4.1. Background

ISO/IEC 20000 standard defines a Service as follows:

A means of delivering value to customers by facilitating outcomes customers want to achieve.

Service-based value extraction enables customers to achieve the outcomes they desire without directly assuming the associated costs and risks.

Service Management is a set of organizational capabilities, which leverage specialized people skills, processes, and technologies, to deliver value to customers in the form of services.

Provider organizations have come to embrace *service frameworks* (e.g. ITIL) for what they deliver—to get clearer and clearer on what they provide to their customers. It is key to BRM relationships with other parts of the Provider organization.

4.4.2. Purpose

Service Management ultimately attempts to improve the definition, delivery and monitoring of services to customers and consumers. It also optimizes those services based upon demand and value.

According to the ISO/IEC 20000 standard, IT Service Management includes:

The design, transition, delivery, and improvement of services that fulfill service requirements and provide value for both the customer and the service Provider. This part of ISO/IEC 20000 requires an integrated process approach when the service Provider plans, establishes, implements, operates, monitors, reviews, maintains, and improves a service management system (SMS).

ISO/IEC 20000 is the first international standard for IT service management. It was developed in 2005, by ISO/IEC JTC1 SC7 and revised in 2011. It is based on and supersedes BS 15000.

4.4.3. Services vs. Products vs. Processes

Products are created and delivered to a consumer as tangible and discernible items produced by an organization. Services, on the other hand, are co-created with their consumer. A service is the production of an essentially intangible benefit, either in its own right or as a significant element of a tangible product. The relationship between a company and its service customers develops gradually, as customers build trust in the company and its ability to deliver on its promises. Service-orientation is a fundamental shift and creates opportunities for new business strategies, new sources of competitive advantage, new ways of interacting with customers, and new ways of organizing work.

A Process is not a service. Processes are linked, linear chains of cause and effect that, when managed carefully, drive predictable, reliable results. Services, on the other hand are co-created with customers each and every time a service is rendered.

4.4.4. Service Value

Service Value is a function of:

- *Utility* (fitness for purpose). Answers the question: "How suitable a given service is for the recipient's intended purpose?" The subjective nature is important: what might be OK for one customer might be completely unacceptable for another.

- *Warranty* (fitness for use). Either an implied or explicit guarantee that the promised utility will be delivered at a given level of consistency.

As an example of service utility, consider Spirit Airline, which promises to deliver the customers safely to their destination at an *ultra-low cost*, but offers few other assurances beyond that. As a result, some customers find Spirit Air's service a great value and a way to travel on tight budget, while others have complained about the virtually non-existent customer service and the frequently encountered rudeness of those customer reps who are available.

The only warranty that Spirit Air effectively provides is that its passengers will arrive safely to their destination—they may, however, depart and arrive later than expected, have to pay extra for luggage and any on-board amenities, etc. These warranty limitations might make Spirit service warranty inadequate for some business travelers and those willing to pay a bit more for additional assurances to arrive on time, at least most of the time, take on a reasonable amount of luggage at no extra cost, and provide a basic set of on-board food and other services, etc.

Characteristics of Service Value

- Value is defined by customers. The ultimate decision about whether the service is valuable or not rests with the customer.

- Affordable mix of features. Customers will select the service or product that represents the best mix of features at the price they are willing to pay.

- Achievement of objectives. Many services are not designed to produce revenue, but to meet some other organizational objective.

- Value changes over time and circumstance. As each customer changes to meet the challenges of their environment, so too do their service needs and values.

Service Value is defined in terms of:

- Business Outcomes
- Perceptions
- Preferences

4.4.5. Service Definition

Eight key questions to be answered when defining a service:

1. What is the service?
2. How do I get the service?
3. How is the service delivered?
4. How do I use the service?
5. How do I get help with the service?
6. What does the service cost?
7. How is the service supported?
8. What does service support cost?

Service definition is key to service management as it enables both the customer and the service Provider to know what to expect and not expect from a service. Clearly defined services enable customers to understand service offerings:

- What a service does and does not include
- Service eligibility
- Service limitations
- Service cost (or price)
- How to request a service
- How to get assistance with a service

A well-defined service identifies internal processes necessary to provide and support that service.

4.4.6. Service Costing

Service Costing is an important aspect in understanding service value:

- Service costing provides critical information required to balance the investment in services across the service portfolio
- Understanding actual costs to serve is a prerequisite to determining benefits realization and ongoing sustainability
- Requires knowledge of the overall service model(s)
- Example costing elements:
  - Direct vs. Indirect Costs
  - Activity Based Costing
  - Fixed vs. Variable Costs
  - CapEx vs. OpEx
- Enterprise Financial Management Policies

4.4.7. Service Risk Management

The service Provider must continually identify, assess and reduce risk within levels of tolerance set by enterprise executive management. This leads to several risk-related service Provider goals:

- IT Compliance and support for business compliance (external laws and regulations)
- Managed IT-related business risk
- Transparency of costs, benefits, and risk
- Security of information, processing infrastructure, and applications
- Delivery of programs delivering benefits, on time, on budget, and meeting requirements and quality standards

4.4.8. Service Provider Constraints

The service Provider has to offer an acceptable service solution that meets the level of warranty and utility to be provided, while accommodating various constraints such as:

- Technology constraints
- Values and ethics at the company
- Copyrights, patents and trademarks pertaining to underlying products and services
- Resource constraints, including schedules
- Compliance with standards and regulations of the company or imposed by external regulators
- Existing commitments
- Comparative unit costs
- Other constraints (policy, government, etc.)

4.4.9. The BRM Role in Service Management

The BRM Role is a crucial link between a service provider and the business acting as a connector, orchestrator, and navigator between the service provider and one or more business units. The BRM role is responsible for stimulating, surfacing, and shaping business demand for a provider's products and services and ensuring that the potential business value from those products and services is captured, optimized, and recognized.

4.5. Portfolio Management

Portfolio Management is a central mechanism for Value Management. The term *portfolio management* is often abused—for example, a *laundry list* of projects is referred to as a portfolio. This is a very dangerous abuse of Portfolio Management concepts and techniques and Business Relationship Management must work hard to position Portfolio Management properly.

4.5.1. Background

Investopedia defines Portfolio Management as:

> The art and science of making decisions about investment mix and policy, matching investments to objectives, asset allocation for individuals and institutions, and balancing risk against performance.

Portfolio Management is based upon Modern Portfolio Theory—a theory of finance developed in the mid-20th Century that attempts to maximize expected return for a given amount of risk, or equivalently minimize risk for a given level of expected return, by carefully choosing the proportions of various assets.

Most of us are familiar with Portfolio Management when applied to our personal investments. For example, it is common to allocate our retirement savings to a mix of *safe* investments (high-quality bonds, for example) and riskier investments such as individual stocks or real estate investments. That mix will change over time (as we move through life stages where putting our children through college is the goal, for example, or saving for retirement) or with changing circumstances (a stock market crash, for example).

When applied to IT investments, IT Portfolio Management is the application of systematic management to large classes of items managed by enterprise IT capabilities. Examples of IT portfolios can include planned initiatives, projects, and ongoing IT services (such as application support), legacy investments, and so on.

The promise of portfolio management includes:

- Ensuring that the portfolio of investments in Provider capabilities and assets represents business strategy.
- The quantification of previously informal Provider efforts, enabling measurement and objective evaluation of investment scenarios.

4.5.2. Purpose

The purpose of Portfolio Management when applied to Provider investments (especially, IT investments) is as a central mechanism to an overall Value Management approach—making investment allocation explicit against strategic choices such as how much to invest in potentially high value, but usually risky initiatives versus safe but low value activities.

4.5.3. Portfolio Management Context

Figure 20 graphically represents how Portfolio Management is central to Value Management. The portfolio allocation decisions represent business strategic intent.

Strategize

For example, a company whose business strategy is to offer globally consistent business processes would chose to invest in a globally common infrastructure. A company who wanted each business unit to be free to innovate and be highly responsive to local circumstances, may be less concerned with a globally common infrastructure and place higher value on local IT investments and local decision making about those investments.

Plan

Strategy (hopefully!) leads to planning, including development of Business Cases and prioritization of investment opportunities. Prioritization and decision making (e.g. business-IT governance) will determine which initiatives are

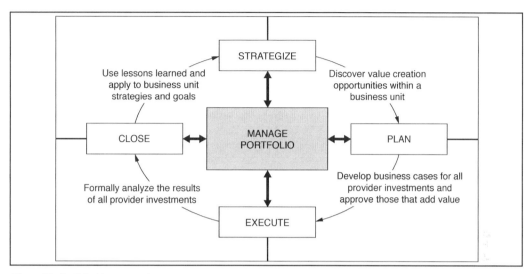

Figure 20 - Portfolio Management

approved for execution (for example, be allocated into this year's portfolio of programs and projects) and which initiatives might be shifted to future years, or which should be put into abeyance for future consideration.

Execute

There will typically be a Portfolio of active projects and programs—these comprise a subset of the total portfolio.

Close

This closes the loop of the Value Management cycle, comparing value realized against value projected for a given asset or initiative.

4.6. Portfolios, Programs and Projects

Figure 21 shows the linkage between Portfolios, Programs and Projects.

Trying to link a project to a portfolio can be difficult for several reasons:

- Projects are often too granular to easily map to a portfolio context.

- Because they tend to be granular, there are frequently too many projects to manage in a strategic way in a portfolio. Trying to sort through and prioritize 100 or so projects is beyond the bandwidth of most prioritization boards!

- Projects are often disconnected from business value – they concern themselves more with budget, schedule and deliverables. As such, they are difficult to map to a portfolio view. As an analogy, most individual investors are pleased to build their investment portfolio from mutual funds (large *baskets* of individual stocks and bonds) rather than buy and track hundreds of individual stocks. In this analogy, the Mutual Fund is the equivalent of a Program.

- Programs connect interdependent projects and are focused on business outcomes. This is much easier to map to the portfolio view than are projects.

So, good portfolio management practice and discipline really demands good program management discipline, which in turn demands good project management discipline.

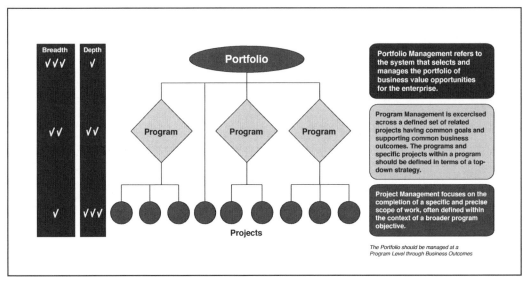

Figure 21 - Relationship between Portfolio, Programs, and Projects

4.6.1. The Investment Context

As shown in Figure 22, Portfolio Management sits between Business Planning (Corporate strategy, investment planning, value realization monitoring) and Program Management (programs of integrated projects, project execution, project/program data collection and reporting, Enterprise Architecture). Planning information flows from Business Planning, through Portfolio Management to Program Management, and Execution information flows from Program Management up to Portfolio Management and then to Business Planning.

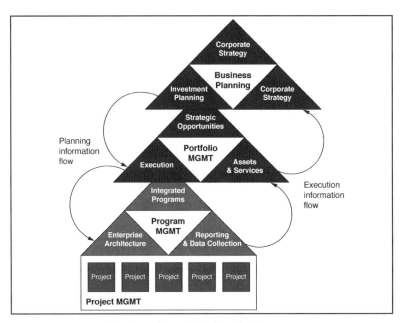

Figure 22 - Investment Planning and Execution Information Flow

4.6.2. Portfolio Management and the Investment Lifecycle

Portfolio Management is applicable when making new investments, managing existing investments, or retiring old investments. Figure 23 shows examples of the different types of portfolio analyses applicable to different stages of the investment lifecycle. Note that Business Planning (see Figure 23) is where Portfolio Strategy should be aligned with business strategy—to reflect the business Strategic Intent.

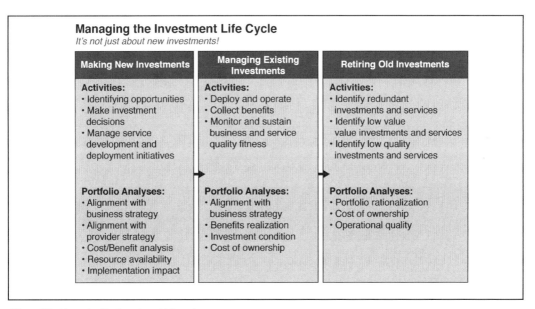

Figure 23 - Managing the Investment Lifecycle

4.6.3. Portfolio Management and the BRM

- Increase business and Provider savvyness around Value Management with Portfolio Management as a central concept

- Use the analogy of Personal Portfolio Management as central to personal wealth, investment and retirement planning

- Compare to changing investment strategies by life stage—putting kids through college, building wealth, planning for retirement, funding retirement, etc.

- Perform simple analysis of current portfolio. Show where the investment goes by asset class. Socialize and ask: "Does this investment pattern align with our business strategies and goals?" "If not, what should the investment pattern look like and how will we move towards that pattern?"

- Help Business Partners understand the cost drivers (especially for steady state services) and what they can do to be *responsible consumers*.

4.7. Portfolio Classification

This paragraph presents two methods of Portfolio Classification for an Information Technology investment portfolio. Once a classification scheme has been defined and agreed, target investment and return levels can be set for each investment and subsequently tracked.

4.7.1. Background

There are many ways to classify IT (or other Provider service) investments, and often multiple views and classifications may be appropriate. For example, spend an hour or so on an investment house website such as Vanguard or Fidelity to see the hundreds of ways finance professionals slice and dice personal investment portfolios.

4.7.2. Purpose

Choosing and implementing one or more Portfolio Classification Schemes is one way to clarify what is of strategic importance to a Business Partner, and is an important contributor to demand shaping and investment prioritization.

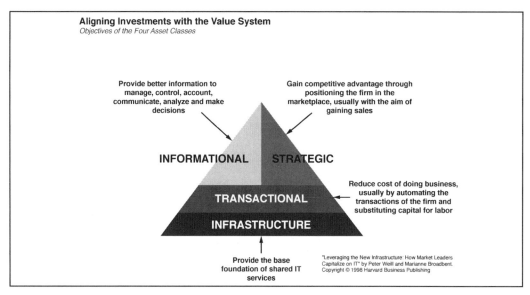

Figure 24 - Weill and Broadbent IT Portfolio Classification Scheme

4.8. Weill/Broadbent Classification Scheme

Figure 24 shows the portfolio classification scheme introduced by Peter Weill and Marianne Broadbent. This popular and relatively simple classification scheme divides the portfolio into four different classes:

4.8.1. Infrastructure

Peter Weill defines infrastructure as, "The base foundation of budgeted-for IT capability (both technical and human), shared throughout the firm as reliable services, and centrally coordinated." This is quite different from the common usage of the term *infrastructure*, but it gets to a powerful and strategic way of thinking about the topic.

Important aspects are:

- Base foundation—implying that all other capability is built upon and depends upon this base. Some people try to cost-justify infrastructure. You really can't. It's the things that infrastructure lets you do that create the value.

- Budgeted-for—implying a level of planning and funding.

- Capability—both human and technical. Infrastructure is so much more than *wires and pipes*.

- Shared throughout the firm—globally common and a shared resource.

- Reliable services—pointing to the concepts of service management.

- Centrally coordinated—not necessarily centrally managed, but certainly centrally coordinated—a necessary aspect of service management and reliable infrastructure.

4.8.2. Transactional

This is often a major part of the portfolio, especially over the last 10-15 years when companies were investing heavily with Enterprise Solutions such as SAP and Oracle. Risks are typically low, and the major justification is cost savings and business process improvement.

4.8.3. Informational

An increasingly important class of investment, capitalizing on the Infrastructure and Transactional systems that have been implemented over the last few years. This class includes the so-called "big data" and business analytics spaces.

4.8.4. Strategic

This class bears the label that is most abused—*strategic* often means "big" or "important to someone's agenda." In reality, *strategic* opportunities should be those that create a competitive advantage that would literally force a competitive response or would force a competitor to fail or lose significant market share. *Strategic* opportunities usually carry high risk.

4.9. The Boston Square

Figure 25 shows the Boston Square, so named because of its roots in the McFarlane/McKenney Strategic Grid, which was introduced in 1983 by McFarlan, McKenney, and Pyburn in the *Harvard Business Review* article "The Information Archipelago—Plotting a Course." Similar in some respects to the Weill/Broadbent classification scheme, the Boston Square suggested different management styles for each class of IT investment.

In its simplest manifestation, the Boston Square uses four classes:

Strategic

Critical to sustain future business strategy, with the primary purpose of gaining competitive advantage.

High Potential

May be important in achieving future business success, but not yet proven, with the primary purpose of gaining competitive advantage.

Factory

Currently depended upon for current business success, with the primary purpose of avoiding competitive disadvantage.

Support

Useful but not critical to current or future success, with the primary purpose of avoiding competitive disadvantage.

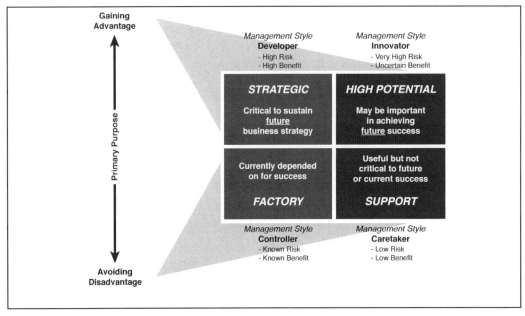

Figure 25 - The Boston Square

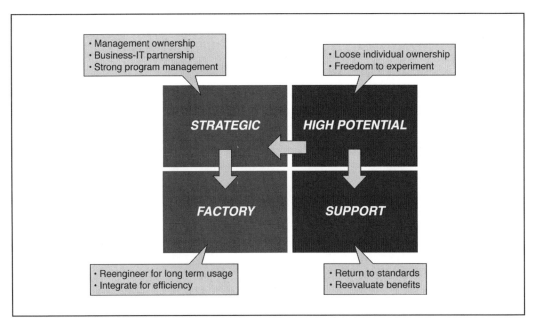

Figure 26 - Moving around the Boston Square

4.9.1. Moving Around the Boston Square

Figure 26 shows how the Boston Square anticipates that investments in one class may move into another class over time. For example, High Potential investments (unproven opportunities) may prove to be Strategic, Support, or just be dropped from the portfolio. Strategic investments may become reclassified as Factory over time—after all, if the investment truly did have strategic impact, competitors must have matched it or trumped it in some way. It is still necessary for running the business, but no longer provides a competitive advantage. An example of this was *yield management* in the airline and eventually, hospitality businesses, where passenger seat (or hotel room) prices are adjusted based upon supply and demand. When first introduced by American Airlines, they gained significant competitive advantage, with several *low-cost* airlines, such as People Express, being put out of business as they were unable to match American's fares in the limited route systems they competed in. Today, all airlines use some form of Yield Management—it's a Factory class investment—a cost of doing business.

4.10. Portfolio Balancing

Portfolio Balancing is a technique that ensures that amounts invested in different Portfolio Asset classes are balanced given the business strategy.

4.10.1. Background

Just as an individual investor periodically assess their allocation across an investment portfolio, and adjusts allocations based upon life stage goals and portfolio performance, so must a business assess their allocation to and return from investments in Provider services, capabilities and assets.

4.10.2. Purpose

A key goal of Portfolio Management is Portfolio Balancing—ensuring that amounts invested in different asset classes are balanced given the business strategy. An individual investor has to rebalance their personal investment portfolio from time to time—for example, when stock and/or bond performance results in the proportion of stocks to bonds shifting beyond what is appropriate given their investment goals and tolerance for risk, or when their investment goals change, say from saving to put children through college to saving for retirement. For an individual investor, Portfolio Balancing might include determining the appropriate balance between low and high risk investments depending upon life stage. A younger individual with a longer investment horizon will typically choose a higher proportion of high risk/potential high return investments (growth stocks, for example) whereas an older individual dependent upon income from their retirement portfolio will typically choose lower risk, lower return investments such as high quality bonds.

Similarly, an enterprise (or business unit) has to revisit their portfolio when business strategy (a major acquisition, or shift in business direction from physical stores to online commerce) or market conditions change (changes in access to capital or cost of capital, for example) or periodically. Portfolio Balancing annually is a good timeframe to consider. For a business, Portfolio Balancing might include increasing the investment in global infrastructure for a company that is shifting to a global strategy. Or increasing its investment in Discovery activities for a company that is looking to become more innovative.

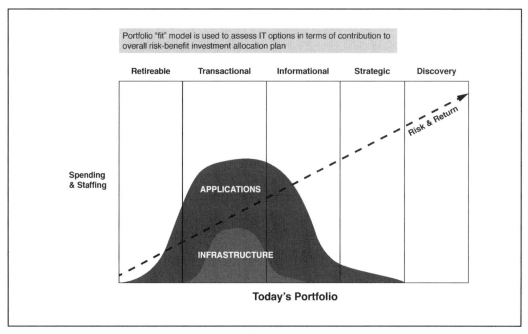

Figure 27 - Example of Portfolio Balancing for Strategic Fit (Current State)

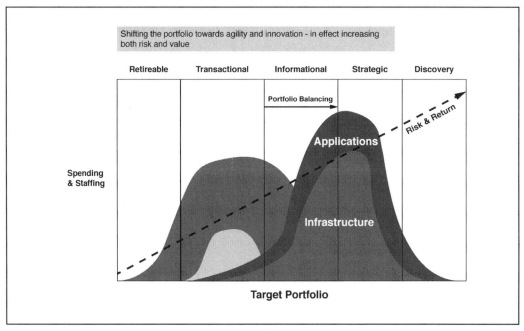

Figure 28 - Example of Portfolio Balancing for Strategic Fit (Target Portfolio)

4.10.3. Example of Portfolio Balancing

Figure 27 is a graphical illustration of typical spending across Portfolio Classes. The total area under the curve equals the total investment.

By analyzing the Current State and determining, for example, that:

- Too much is being spent on Applications (due to redundancy as a result of failing to rationalize investments after a series of acquisitions that were not integrated)
- Not enough is being spent on Infrastructure (which could provide a platform for greater sharing, collaboration and communication across the enterprise)
- Too much is being spent on technology that should have been retired (e.g. its functionality is duplicated in newer capabilities)
- Not enough being spent on Strategic Opportunities (that would enhance the firm's competitive position)
- Nothing is being spent on Discovery that might find innovation opportunities that could better differentiate the firm

Portfolio Balancing would define a new Portfolio Strategy that better matches the firm's strategic intent, for example (Figure 28):

- Increase Infrastructure spending (establishing a globally common infrastructure, for example)
- Decrease applications spending (e.g. replacing 12 different enterprise systems with a single instance)
- Eliminate *retireable* investments to free up money and resources for higher value activities
- Move investment and resources towards Informational and Strategic opportunities
- Allocating resources for Discovery activities

Figure 29 illustrates a typical Portfolio Management Lifecycle and the major activities in each phase.

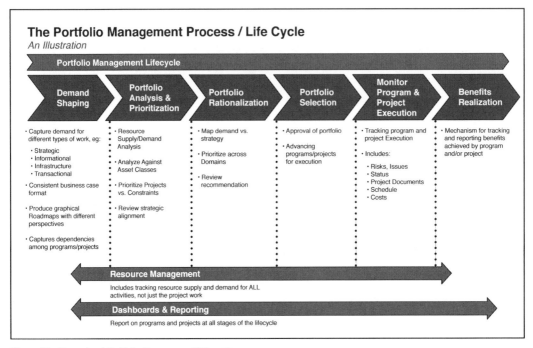

Figure 29 - Example of Portfolio Management Lifecycle

4.10.4. Portfolio Management and the BRM

- Increase business and Provider savvyness around Value Management with Portfolio Management as a central concept

- Use the analogy of Personal Portfolio Management as central to personal wealth, investment and retirement planning

- Compare to changing investment strategies by life stage – putting kids through college, building wealth, planning for retirement, funding retirement, etc.

- Perform simple analysis of current portfolio. Show where the investment goes by asset class. Socialize and ask: "Does this investment pattern align with our business strategies and goals?" "If not, what should the investment pattern look like and how will we move towards that pattern?"

- Help Business Partners understand the cost drivers (especially for steady state services) and what they can do to be *responsible consumers*.

5. Techniques

5.1. Business Capability Roadmapping

Business Capability Roadmapping is an approach to aligning Business and IT strategies and imperatives.

Value

- Capability conversations increase business acumen
- Encourages strategic versus project thinking
- Roadmap analysis reveals cross-enterprise opportunities to deploy capabilities smarter and faster—cross-BRM collaboration is essential
- Maps supply insights into provider direction and skill planning
- Drives a multi-year vision of the capability at which the company must excel

5.1.1. Background

Business Capability Roadmapping is a way to clarify Business Capabilities needed to implement business strategy and the Provider Capabilities needed to enable those Business Capabilities. There are various methodologies and tools available—some proprietary—to support Business Capabilities Roadmapping, including the CEB's IT Roadmap Builder and the Albright Strategy Group's Capability Roadmapping.

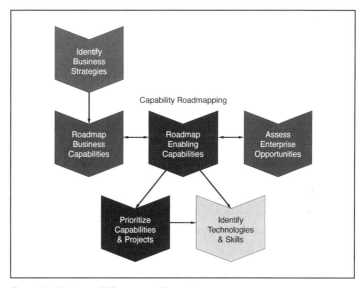

Figure 30 - Business IT Governance Example

5.1.2. Purpose

Business Capability Roadmapping offers a number of important characteristics and benefits:

- Lays out where the business is taking key capabilities over the next 2-3 years to support its strategic objectives.
- Aligns business process, information, application and technology capabilities to a common plan.
- Facilitates strategic thinking versus short-term project thinking.
- Drives conversations that help increase both business and Provider savvyness.
- Roadmap analysis reveals cross-enterprise opportunities to deploy capabilities smarter and faster.
- Maps supply insights into Provider technology direction and workforce planning.

Business Capability Roadmapping is the crucial set of steps that links from Business Strategy Formulation to IT Project Initiation.

5.1.3. Role of the BRM

- Ensure that Business Strategy is translated into a Business Capability Roadmap
- Orchestrate key provider resources to be involved in Business Capability Roadmap development
  e.g. Project Managers, Enterprise Architects, Business Analysts, and Strategists
- Ensure that key business partner resources are involved in and take ownership for the Business Capability Roadmap
  e.g. Executive Leadership, Process Owners, and Subject Matter Experts
- Help communicate and socialize the drafts and final results
- Consider and incorporate the wider enterprise implications
  e.g. Business Transition Management issues

5.1.4. Capability Categories

Business Capability

Business capability is the expression or the articulation of the capacity, materials and expertise an organization needs in order to perform core functions. Enterprise architects use business capabilities to illustrate the overarching needs of the business in order to better strategize Provider solutions that meet those business needs.

A Business Capability can be thought of as the activities a business must perform in order to exist/operate. These are independent of the organization structure, technology and not in a specific sequence. It can be helpful to think of business capabilities in the context of sentences such as, "The Ability to do..." or "Excellence in..." Business Capabilities is the what, not the how of business activity.

Common examples of Business Capability include:

- Drive Brand Equity
- Manage Customer Relationships
- Drive Acquisition Integrations

Enabling IT Capability

An Provider Capability can be thought of as everything it takes behind the scenes that makes an provider service possible. This will include:

- One or more Processes.

- Descriptions of the Roles needed to perform one or more of the procedures within a process (e.g. Project Manager, Business Analyst, and Relationship Manager).

- Descriptions of the Competencies needed to perform a given role (what the person performing the role needs to know, e.g. business knowledge, what skills they need, e.g. facilitation, and what behaviors they should exhibit, e.g. results orientation).

- An adequate supply of competent human resources filling the given roles.

- Tools and technologies needed to automate or execute necessary processes or procedures.

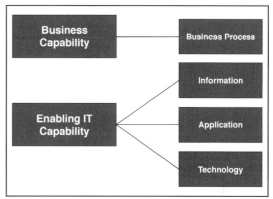

Figure 31 - Capabilities Categories

- Management systems necessary to ensure the health and performance of the Capability, including funding, organizational will, personal incentives, and so on.

In the context of Business Capability Roadmapping, we can simplify Enabling IT Capability as comprising Information, Applications, and Technology.

5.1.5. Business Capability Roadmapping Process

Business Capability Roadmapping typically follows a 7-step process as outlined in Figure 32

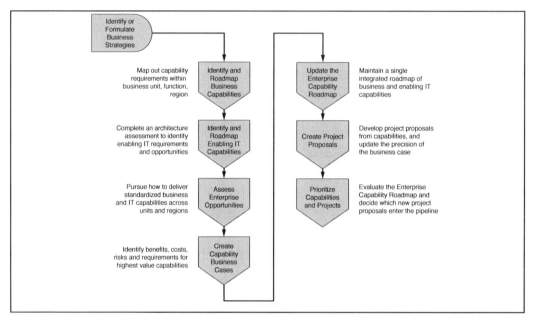

Figure 32 - Business Capability Roadmapping Process

5.2. Linking Business Drivers with Technology

This technique links a Business Partner's Business Drivers with Technology and illustrates the distinctions between Solution Based and Value Based discussions between a Provider and their Business Partner.

5.2.1. Background

Linking IT capabilities with business strategy is a perennial challenge involving many different types of conversations among various stakeholders leading to a complex set of business and IT decisions. Sometimes, those discussions are based upon business problems and the technology needed to address them. Other times they are based upon the technology solutions available, how these might address specific business problems. This page illustrates those two types of discussion and how to use each.

5.2.2. Purpose

Having a clearer sense of the two types of conversation—solution based and value based discussions—can help the BRM know when and how to approach a given business situation. It can also help integrate the perspectives of the strategist, architect and product/platform manager.

5.2.3. Types of Discussion that Link Business Needs to Technology Solutions

Figure 33 illustrates the linkage between Business Drivers (the business "what"), Business Initiatives (the business "how"), IT Enablers (the IT "what"), and Technology (the IT "how").

- Business Drivers
  These are the key business outcomes the Business Partner needs to achieve.

- Business Initiatives
  These are the projects, programs, and actions the Business Partner will have to undertake in order to create the business outcomes.

- IT Enablers
  These are the IT capabilities needed to enable the Business Initiatives.

- Technology
  This is the technology required to provide the IT enablers.

- Solution Based Discussions
  These begin with the solution and try to find how this solution may address a given business problem. There is nothing inherently wrong with this type of conversation, but it may not be the best starting point in the Business Partner-BRM dialog. Starting from the solution tends to sound as though IT is trying to force a technology onto a business problem—whether it is the best solution or not!

- Value Based Discussions
  These start with the business problem or the business outcomes to be achieved. A Value Based discussion is nearly always the preferred approach, even if it ultimately leads to a Solution Based discussion.

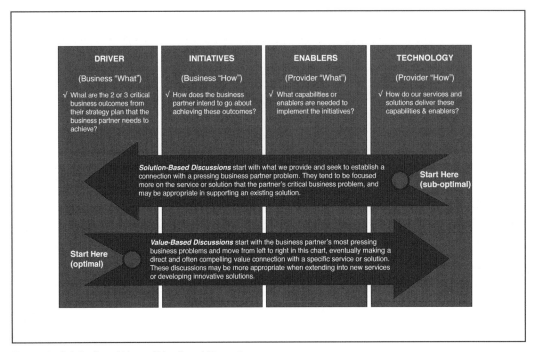

Figure 33 - Solution Based Versus Value Based Discussions

5.3. Value Management

Value Management ties together into a holistic and comprehensive approach the concepts of Ideation, Value Planning, Portfolio Management and the Business Case to capture, optimize and communicate the business value of Provider investments and capabilities.

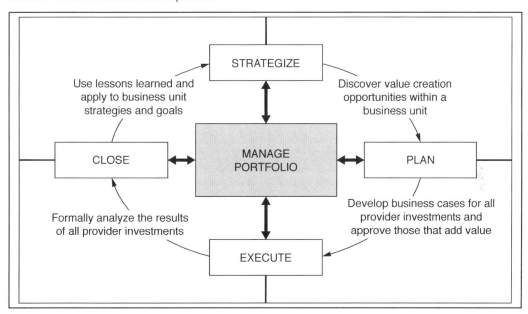

Figure 34 - Value Management Framework

5.3.1. Background

Value Management is the process of defining, measuring, optimizing and communicating the net value of a Provider investment over time.

Value Management recognizes the contribution of a Provider investment to an organization's strategic and operational objectives. It incorporates activities associated with:

- Ideation—strategizing to surface potential initiatives to create business value.
- Value Planning—identifying the Business Drivers and Key Performance Indicators that will be impacted by a given initiative, how they will be impacted, and how they will be reported.
- Business Case—detailed justification for all costs and benefits associated with a given initiative.
- Optimization—Review the planned value versus actual value after implementation and adjust as needed to ensure maximum return on value.

Value Management is best approached as an extension to the Systems Development Life Cycle (SDLC).

5.3.2. Purpose

Value Management is used to:

- Identify initiatives that have the potential to create business value by positively impacting Business Drivers
- Ensure that value is delivered by tracking progress against investment targets
- Assist with priority setting for Provider investments
- Evaluate competing investment opportunities
- Avoid making the wrong investments
- Link compensation to value management
- Optimize the value realized in practice once a business solution or service is deployed

When is Value Management Applied?

Typically there are thresholds above which Value Management is applied (e.g. IT investments of $100,000 and above), but it is good discipline to use Value Management on most projects.

Value Management can be used every time a project authorization or "go/no-go" decision is made (regardless of the size of the project). It can also be used during and after project implementation, to monitor and audit project success.

5.4. The Value Management Process

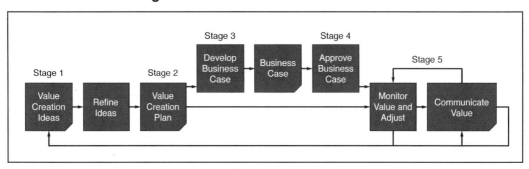

Figure 35 - Value Management Process

The Value Management Process, illustrated in Figure 35, tracks investments from the opportunity identification stage through delivery and operation. It comprises 5 major stages:

1. Capture Value Ideas: This stage examines ideas/possibilities for business value. Its output is an Idea Document.

2. Create Value Plan: This stage creates a plan for the value to be realized if the idea/possibility is pursued. Its output is a Value Creation Plan.

3. Create Business Case: This stage completes a business case for all investments above a certain threshold.

4. Approve Business Case: This stage analyzes submitted business cases, and approves them based upon their merit in terms of NPV and the strength of the case, and relative to other investments that are competing for resources.

5. Capture and Communicate Value: This stage executes the Value Plan to track, audit and communicate the actual value generated versus the value forecast in the business case and to optimize the value delivered in the light of experience.

5.4.1. Stage 1 - Capture Value Opportunities

Value can be described as the net difference a proposed change creates in the business performance which results in financial, operational or strategic benefit. A description of the value opportunity is a key input to the Value Plan and to a decision to proceed with a business case. The ultimate decision to proceed with a business case is based on the alignment of the value opportunity with strategic business objectives (identified in the Business Strategy.)

The key deliverable from Stage 1 is the Idea Document detailed below. This is meant to be a very high-level overview description of the idea and should be completed in a very short amount of time.

Idea Document

1. Name of the Idea/Opportunity.

2. Identify key stakeholders who would benefit from or be impacted if the idea/opportunity were pursued.

3. Define the Idea/Opportunity.
What Business Driver(s) are impacted, how are they impacted and why are they impacted?
What is the business problem to be solved or opportunity to be pursued?
What is the Business Vision or Future State if the problem were to be solved or the opportunity pursued?
What is the value to the business if the problem was solved or opportunity pursued?

4. Define the consequences if the problem is not solved or the opportunity not pursued.

5. What business process(es) will be changed and how will they be changed?

6. What, at a high-level, is the Organizational Change Management Plan, including key initiating and sustaining sponsors, enablers, barriers, and impacted change targets.

7. What would be the high-level features and functions.
In Scope?
Out of scope?
Major Assumptions?
Major Constraints

8. Approvals to move forward

5.4.2. Stage 2 - Create Value Plan

The Value Plan identifies how business value will be created and monitored if the idea/opportunity is pursued. It does this based upon the Business Value Drivers and the specific Business Outcomes that will be impacted.

The key deliverable from Stage 2 is the Value Plan detailed below.

Value Plan

For each impacted Business Outcome, define the seven elements below:

1. Definition

2. Value by timeframe

3. Reporting Schedule

4. How measured

5. How long will the value be measured

6. Stakeholders and their level of commitment

7. Point of action

5.4.3. Stage 3 - Develop Business Case

We develop a Business Case in order to:

- Identify the strategic alignment and urgency of the proposed project or to document the regulatory or legal requirements for implementing the project.
- Justify pursuing an investment that will satisfy strategic business objectives and goals.
- Acquire full commitment by all stakeholders involved.
- Communicate a comprehensive value proposition in terms of a project's cost-benefit analysis, alignment with business objectives, stakeholders and risks.
- Support the decision making process and to facilitate Portfolio Management.
- Identify how to measure value that will be created by a project.

The impact of the investment should dictate who contributes to the development of the Business Case, using factors such as where the costs and benefits are incurred or realized as a result of the investment:

- One business unit?
- Multiple business units?
- Common Services (e.g. infrastructure)?
- Change in allocation

See Business Case Components for suggestions of what an effective Business Case should contain.

5.4.4. Stage 4 - Approve Business Case

The process for approving Business Cases is called the Approval Roadmap.

Typical Business Case Evaluation Criteria

Business Case Merit

- Is the business case compelling (e.g. does it satisfy a stated BU strategy)?
- Is the relative NPV positive (or the business case serves a mandate)?
- Success can be a *no-go* decision

Competing Opportunities

- Budget and resource constraints
- Higher value opportunities
- Same NPV, but different benefit mix
- Internal Rate of Return (IRR) and Payback Period may be useful to compare alternatives

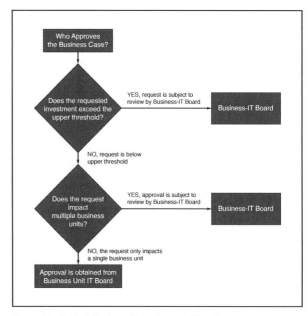

Figure 36 - Typical Business Case Approval Roadmap

Portfolio Considerations

- Types of Provider investments (Portfolio Classification)
- Predetermined mix of types
- Evaluation nuances by type
- Contribution (or detraction) from Infrastructure
- Compliance with existing standards and platforms

5.4.5. Stage 5 - Capture and Communicate Value

The actual improvements in performance indicators must be measured, recorded and tracked in order to:

- Monitor progress.
- Receive early warning of potential problems with achieving project success.
- Validate and/or improve project planning and implementation processes.
- Validate and/or adjust benefits received by stakeholders.

The measurement of value is done by executing the Value Measurement Plan documented in the business case.

Reasons to Capture Value

- Ensure user adoption of new processes or systems
- Changes in the environment (regulatory, legal, economic, etc.), as well as internal company changes and project implementation problems, may be a cause to take action:
  - Action may involve providing additional or different resources to the project, in order to assist with its successful implementation.
  - Action may also involve termination or suspension of the project in order to cap losses:
    - Only future cash flows, not sunk costs, matter in decision making.
    - The ability to terminate or suspend projects is one of the key managerial tools.
  - Being able to properly react to changes is one of the greatest benefits of capturing value.
- Communicating the value created encourages future value creating behavior.
  - Communicating value created should be done throughout the organization:
    - To recognize those individuals who made the success possible.
    - To demonstrate and encourage future value creating behavior.
    - To institutionalize value management in the organization's culture.
  - The CIO Value Management Staff plays an important role in value capture and communication by:
    - Analyzing and maintaining the IT portfolio.
    - Producing regular portfolio and value classes, presentations, and reports.

5.5. Business Value Leakage

Business Value Leakage occurs when the full Potential Value from solving a business problem or exploiting an opportunity is not realized in practice. Value leaks when the Value System between Provider and Business Partner is misaligned; when opportunities to create value are missed, when Provider solutions fail to fully meet the needs of the opportunity, when the solution is deployed or operated in a suboptimal way, or when business value measurement, accountability or organizational capability are lacking.

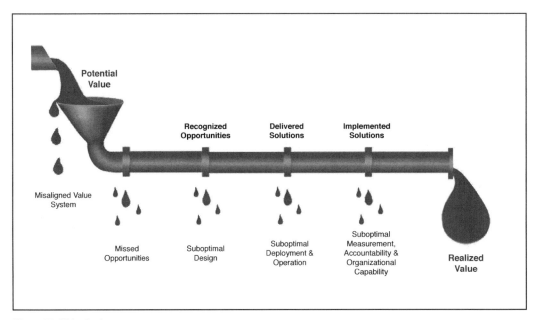

Figure 37 - Value Leakage

5.5.1. Common Sources of Value Leakage

It is useful to think about business value as something that flows through a pipeline. Note, in Figure 37 that the pipeline flows uphill (extracting value always seems to be an uphill struggle, working against the forces of gravity and momentum)! Also note that the pipeline leaks—some potential value is never realized!

Misaligned Value System

Value Systems are usually implicit and vary by stakeholder. For one stakeholder, the Value System might revolve around innovation and new revenue sources. For another stakeholder, it might have more to do with taking out costs or improving cycle time for product development. Sometimes, the Value System of the Provider is mismatched with that of the Business Partner. For example, the Provider might value fully featured, technologically advanced business solutions, designed to meet all possible needs and to last a long time. The Business Partner, on the other hand, might be looking for a 'quick and dirty' solution to a short-term business problem.

Business Relationship Management has to gain clarity about the Business Partner's Value System and ensure that Provider actions and investments appeal to that Value System.

The Misaligned Value System is a result of the Contextual Barrier we discussed in the Business-Provider Alignment model.

Missed Opportunities

Opportunities to create business value are easily missed—they can go unrecognized, or recognized but not exploited sufficiently quickly to yield the potential results.

Business Relationship Management must work to constantly stimulate, surface and shape business demand by recognizing and suggesting opportunities that the Business Partner may not have recognized.

Missed Opportunities result from, among other things, the Expression Barrier in the Business-Provider Alignment model.

Suboptimal Design

When solutions or services fail to meet the needs of the Business Partner due to flawed design (which can include missing functionality, features that are hard to use or to discover, over-design and too much complexity) then value leaks.

Business Relationship Management must ensure that the service or solution design will create the intended key Business Outcomes.

Suboptimal Design results from the Specification Barrier in the Business-Provider Alignment model.

Suboptimal Deployment and Operation

Sometimes, value is lost in the way the solution or service is deployed. Examples include inadequate or ineffective training, poor management of organizational change (Business Transition Management), and failure to replace obsolete solutions when new solutions are available (people continue using the old, familiar solution rather than learn the new solution).

Business Relationship Management must keep deployment focused on the Business Outcomes, and ensure a Program Management perspective (i.e. the solution is not complete until it is being used and delivering on its intended goals).

Suboptimal Deployment and Operation result from, among other things, the Implementation Barrier in the Business-Provider Alignment model.

Suboptimal Measurement, Accountability and Organizational Capability

Failure to measure the realized value is a very common source of leakage. There are several reasons for this:

1. Failure to identify what the value measures should be and how to measure them frequently means failure to clarify the purposes and goals of a given service or solution. In other words, the act of identifying value measures and metrics creates opportunities for confusion about needed functionality, business process change, training needs, needs to change performance management systems, etc.

2. Failure to identify what the value measures should be often means failure to understand implications for organizational capability (both the Provider's and the Business Partner's) leading to gaps in organizational capability that inhibit the value being realized.

3. Failure to measure realized value means you don't know how well a solution or service is working, or how to make it work more effectively.

4. Failure to measure realized value means you can't hold anyone accountable for that value. If nobody is accountable, there's a good chance the value will not be realized.

5. Failure to measure realized value means you have no basis to understand how to tune and optimize the solution or service.

6. Failure to measure realized value means you don't know when the costs of a solution or service exceed the delivered value and that solution should be retired.

Suboptimal Measurement, Accountability and Organizational Capability are results of the Contextual Barrier we discussed in the Business-Provider Alignment model.

5.6. Business Outcomes

Business Outcomes are a means to establishing a discipline of value—from clarifying an opportunity, through to managing scope, establishing focus and ownership, through to measuring and optimizing realized value.

5.6.1. Background

"Begin with the end in mind" is the second of the late Stephen Covey's *7 Habits of Highly Effective People*. It is also a great way to summarize the discipline of value's emphasis on Business Outcomes.

5.6.2. Purpose

Business Outcomes are a way of clarifying strategic intents by driving down from what are often vague goals (e.g. increase sales) to something far more specific and tangible. As such, clarity of business outcomes can help achieve:

- Refinement of ideas and opportunities for ways to leverage information and IT
- Clarification of business needs
- Clarification of Business Strategy
- Definition and management of scope for business-IT initiatives
- Mapping potential solutions against needs
- Determining value measures
- Measuring value
- Optimizing the value realized through business-IT initiatives
- Identifying priorities across competing initiatives
- Reaching benefit realization decisions
- Business Outcomes Approach

5.6.3. Business Outcomes Approach

Figure 38 represents a very high level 4-stage process:

Develop Outcomes

Business Outcomes focus on results, not a process or procedure. Strong business outcomes have the following characteristics:

- Important to the business
- Provide a definition of success from the business perspective
- Represent the results to be obtained, not the process for attaining it
- Allow you to focus on the critical few
- Map to significant business value, ultimately leading to increased revenue, reduced costs, or enhanced shareholder value
- Visible and unambiguous (e.g. we deliver products on time—or we don't)
- Each Business Outcome is discrete—you can decide to include it or reject it
- They help you see the detail, but not wallow in it

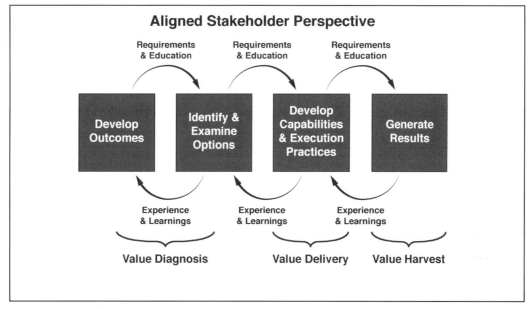

Figure 38 - Business Outcomes Approach

- They are translatable into "effect on me"
- Operationally specific and measurable – you know when you have successfully achieved a given Business Outcome
- Strategic or financial outcomes like customer satisfaction must be translated into operational outcomes like on-time delivery with no defects
- Can be clearly articulated as levels of performance
- The most important Business Outcomes tend to be those that have an external market impact

Business Outcomes Share Characteristics With SMART Goals

SMART (or, sometimes S.M.A.R.T.) is popular acronym in management literature. Unfortunately, a search of the literature reveals several variations on what the letters stand for. Common variations include:

- **S**pecific
  - Who is involved?
  - What do I want to accomplish?
  - Where (identify a location)?
  - When (establish a time frame)?
  - Which (identify requirements and constraints)?
  - Why (specific reasons, purpose or value derived from accomplishing the goal)?

- **M**easurable
    - Establish concrete criteria for measuring progress
    - How much (how will I know when it is accomplished)?
- **A**ttainable/Assignable/Achievable
- **R**ealistic/Relevant/Results-focused
    - A goal must represent an objective toward which you are both willing and able to work.
- **T**imely/Time-bound

Example of Strong Business Outcomes

Strong Business Outcomes Examples	Weak Outcomes Examples
Increase wholesale distribution revenues by $1.2 billion in 2014	Enhance value and revenues in the newly acquired generation assets
Optimize XYZ Station Operations, reducing outage time by 10%	Streamline and Optimize Operations
Reduce fossil fuel costs by 10%, after tax by FY end 2014	Reduce Operating Costs
Develop a "real-time" inventory system to decrease cycle time by 10% and reduce carrying costs by 30% over the next 12 months	Improve on-time order delivery and inventory management processes

Table 1 - Strong vs. Weak Business Outcomes Examples

Determining Business Outcomes and Measures

Examine Issues

- What are the major business strategies of the corporation?
- What are the major issues, business and technical, to be addressed?
- Where is business value not being realized?
- What are implications of these issues to costs, growth, market share?

Identify Outcomes

- What business outcome would solve each issue?
- How would the outcome solve the issue?

Identify Impacts

- What is the impact to the business of each outcome?
- What is the potential value to the business of each outcome?
- Which outcomes are most important to the business?

Determine Measures

- How could you measure the outcome?
- What are the specific measurements of each outcome?

Identify and Examine Options

Once the major Business Outcomes have been determined, you are then in a position to examine options for achieving those outcomes, and to select the most attractive option. Developing Business Outcomes and identifying options for realizing those outcomes together comprise Value Diagnosis.

Develop Capabilities and Execution Practices

Once the most attractive option has been selected, you can develop needed business, technology and other capabilities that will enable the achievement of the Business Outcomes. During this stage, the targeted Business Outcomes should serve as a constant filter to help manage scope. Any new requirement that surfaces should be challenged—"Are there any Business Outcomes that would be compromised if we don't address the new requirement?" If there are no Business Outcomes that would be compromised by omission of the new requirement, then that requirement should be either dropped, or postponed until such time as it is essential for value realization. Developing capabilities and execution practices is the key to Value Delivery.

Generate Results

Once the capabilities have been deployed and the associated execution practices put in place, results are generated and compared against the Business Outcomes that had been planned. Capabilities and execution practices can then be *tuned* in the light of practice and performance against targeted Business Outcomes. Generating results is where value is harvested.

5.7. Customer Value Hierarchy

The Customer Value Hierarchy (CVH) is a technique for discovering the needs and value expectations of an individual Business Partner. Used correctly, it allows the Team to not only identify the specific needs of the Business Partner, but also to categorize those needs into three levels of criticality.

5.7.1. Background

The Customer Value Hierarchy is based upon the *Kano Model* which is a theory of product development and customer satisfaction developed in the 1980s by Professor Noriaki Kano. The Kano Model classifies customer preferences into five categories.

1. Attractive Quality: These attributes provide satisfaction when achieved fully, but do not cause dissatisfaction when not fulfilled. These are attributes that are not normally expected, For example, a thermometer on a package of milk showing the temperature of the milk. Since these types of attributes of quality unexpectedly delight customers, they are often unspoken.

2. One-dimensional Quality: These attributes result in satisfaction when fulfilled and dissatisfaction when not fulfilled. These are attributes that are spoken of and ones which companies compete for. An example of this would be a milk package that is said to have ten percent more milk for the same price will result in customer satisfaction, but if it only contains six percent then the customer will feel misled and it will lead to dissatisfaction.

3. Must-be Quality: These attributes are taken for granted when fulfilled but result in dissatisfaction when not fulfilled. An example of this would be package of milk that leaks. Customers are dissatisfied when the package leaks, but when it does not leak the result is not increased customer satisfaction. Since customers expect these attributes and view them as basic, it is unlikely that they are going to tell the company about them when asked about quality attributes.

4. Indifferent Quality: These attributes refer to aspects that are neither good nor bad, and they do not result in either customer satisfaction or customer dissatisfaction.

5. Reverse Quality: These attributes refer to a high degree of achievement resulting in dissatisfaction and to the fact that not all customers are alike. For example, some customers prefer high-tech products, while others prefer the basic model of a product and will be dissatisfied if a product has too many extra features.

The Customer Value Hierarchy simplifies the Kano Model into three categories:

1. Table Stakes
2. Satisfiers
3. Differentiators

5.7.2. Purpose

The Customer Value Hierarchy offers insights into product or services attributes which are perceived to be important to customers. The purpose of the technique is to support the specification of products and services and raise the quality of discussion through better development of team understanding. The model focuses on differentiating product or service features, rather than focusing initially on customer needs.

5.7.3. Customer Value Hierarchy Model

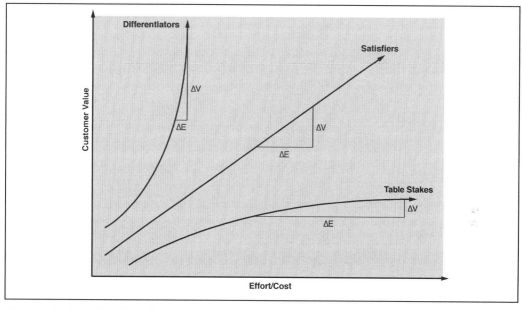

Figure 39 - Customer Value Hierarchy

Table Stakes (Got-to-Have Expectations)

Table Stakes represent the essential needs of the Business Partner, without which, meeting the higher order value expectations may not be meaningful or palpable. An important characteristic of Table Stakes expectations is that they operate as threshold expectations: once the expectation is met, there is little benefit associated with over-investing and exceeding expectations of this type.

In the IT domain, Table Stakes would include such things as:

- Acceptable service and solution reliability and functionality
- Attractive Value/Price Relationship (ROI)
- Confidence in the Provider's development process and product roadmap

Satisfiers (Want-to-Have Expectations)

Satisfiers represent services and products which may be normally expected from a Provider, but without which the Business Partner can live. Examples include:

- Proactively identify additional opportunities for value creation
- Drive revenue growth, not just cost reduction
- Participation in product trajectory and definition of product or service roadmap

Differentiators (Wow! Expectations)

Differentiators always involve an element of surprise, and have the greatest impact on a Business Partner perception of value creation. Examples include:

- Introductions to strategic partners to whom the Business Partner would not otherwise have access
- Accelerate key business transformation initiatives
- Drive quantum change in business performance

5.7.4. Application Notes

Context Setting

Objectives

"We are committed to working on our relationships with our Business Partners so that together we consistently create value for the enterprise. The first step in that exercise is to make sure that we understand and prioritize those things that are most important to you."

Approach

"We use a framework that identifies three types of needs or expectations that you may have, as shown on this chart. This conversation will focus on understanding your needs and expectations, but I cannot make any commitments about what we can or will do. In our next meeting, I will make sure that I have this information correct, and will agree with you on our priorities for the next year."

Validation

- Ensure that your Business Partner agrees with how you have characterized their value hierarchy (showing them the draft).
- Agree on their view of the extent to which each value expectation has been fulfilled, placing the assessment in the box in the upper right of the cell.
- Ensure that the level (*got-to-have, want-to-have,* and *wow*) is appropriately defined.

Alignment

After having discussed with the Business Partner service team:

- Be clear about what can be addressed and what cannot be addressed (expectations management)
- Agree with the customer on prioritization

Customer Needs Interview - Example Questions

- Think about your best internal or external Business Partners. What is it about those relationships that really makes a difference to your operation?
- I know that we are generally meeting the terms of our SLA/contract. What else should we be focusing on to improve performance?
- What other things do we need to pay attention to? How are we doing in those areas now?
- Of all the people in your organization who follow our performance or know about our work here, who has the least favorable impression? Why is that? What could we do to improve that?
- We'd like to be so highly regarded that you'd be telling your partners about us. Is there anything that prevents you from doing that now?
- What is the next opportunity that we should be thinking about here? What do we need to do for that to be a huge win for you?
- Where do you see your next position in the company? What do you need to accomplish in order to achieve that objective?

5.7.5. Example Results from Completing Customer Value Hierarchy Discovery

Got to Have Expectations	Want to Have Expectations	Wow! Expectations
No surprises! If there is a problem, I want to hear about it first hand, not through back channels. **M**	Provide timely advice and counsel when needed not just when asked. **M**	Offer creative ideas to improve our competitive position and create new customer relationships. **D**
Trust & loyalty - I need to know that my business partner is furthering my best interests and advocating on my behalf. **D**	Understand my priorities and initiate creative suggestions for growing the business. **D**	Make introductions for me to interesting business partners. **D**
Serve as solution partner, selecting the best option for my business and the firm as a whole. **E**	Consolidate four seperate financial systems into no more than 2 (retail, wholesale). **D**	Demonstrate how emerging technologies are being used by potential competitors and how we could use them to enhance our competitive position. **D**

D Deficient

M Meets

E Exceeds

Figure 40 - Example Customer Value Hierarchy Analysis

In the example shown in Figure 40, the BRM has completed and validated an analysis of the Business Partner's needs and expectations in each category and has determined which needs and expectations are deficient, met or exceeded. This provides the input to the Diagnosing Relationship Quality technique.

5.8. Diagnosing Relationship Quality

The Diagnosing Relationship Quality technique helps determine the strength of a BRMs relationship with their Business Partner.

5.8.1. Background

The Diagnosing Relationship Quality technique is used by BRMs as part of Strategic Relationship Management. It is used in conjunction with the Building Customer Value Hierarchy and Building a Relationship Improvement Plan techniques. It is applied for each key Business Partner relationship of the BRM.

5.8.2. Purpose

The Diagnosing Relationship Quality technique is used to determine the strength of a Provider's relationship with a Business Partner based upon the degree to which expectations discovered using the Customer Value Hierarchy are met.

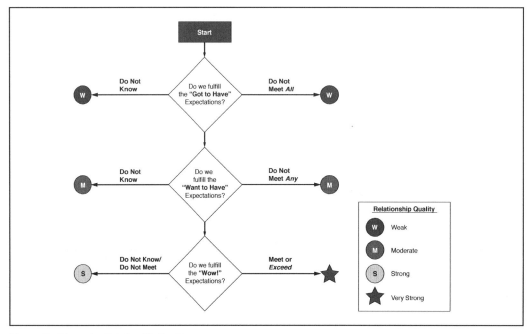

Figure 41 - Diagnosing Relationship Quality

5.8.3. Using the Diagnosing Relationship Quality Technique

Work though the 3 steps as indicated in Figure 41 and post the results to the Relationship Value Map.

5.8.4. Step 1

Step 1 asks, "Do we fulfill the *got-to-have* expectations?"

1. If we do not know, or are unsure of the answer, then we have a Weak relationship with our Business Partner, and need to invest time in the Discovery step of the Strategic Relationship Management process to determine why.

2. If we know the answer, and that answer is that we do not meet all *got-to-have* expectations, then the relationship is also Weak but in this case we need to use Discovery to determine why those expectations are not being met, and what can be done to meet them.

3. If we know the answer, and that answer is that we do meet or exceed all *got-to-have* expectations, then the relationship is of Moderate strength and we can use Discovery to examine the degree to which we are satisfying *want-to-have* expectations.

5.8.5. Step 2

Step 2 asks, "Do we fulfill the *want-to-have* expectations?"

1. If we do not know, or are unsure of the answer, then we have a Moderate relationship with our Business Partner, and need to invest time in the Discovery step of the Strategic Relationship Management process to determine why.

2. If we know the answer, and that answer is that we do not meet any *want-to-have* expectations, then the relationship is also Moderate but in this case we need to use Discovery to determine why those expectations are not being met, and what can be done to meet them.

3. If we know the answer, and that answer is that we do meet or exceed some *want-to-have* expectations, then the relationship is Strong and we can use Discovery to examine the degree to which we are satisfying *wow* expectations.

5.8.6. Step 3

Step 3 asks, "Do we fulfill the *wow* expectations?"

1. If we do not know, or do not meet the *wow* expectations, then we have a Strong relationship with our Business Partner, and need to invest time in the Discovery step of the Strategic Relationship Management process to determine why.

2. If we know the answer, and that answer is that we do meet or exceed the *wow* expectations, then the relationship is Very Strong and we work to expand the relationship.

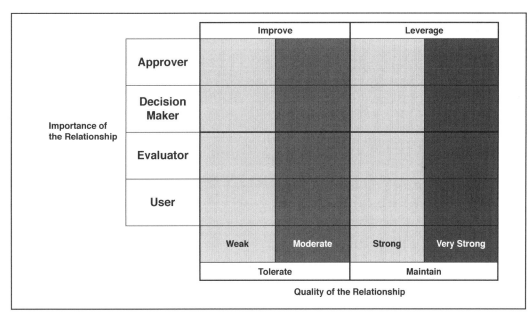

Figure 42 - Relationship Value Map

5.9. Relationship Value Mapping technique.

5.9.1. Purpose

The Relationship Value Mapping technique helps clarify the importance of a given relationship (the vertical dimension in Figure 42). With this information, the quality of each relationship, as determined using the Diagnosing Relationship Quality technique (the horizontal dimension in Figure 42), can be plotted to create an overall picture of relationship importance against relationship quality. This provides the key inputs to Relationship Improvement Planning.

5.9.2. Using the Relationship Quality Diagnostic

The map is divided into four quadrants—Improve, Leverage, Tolerate, and Maintain. Weak or Moderate relationships can be Tolerated or Improved, while Strong or Very Strong relationships can be maintained or leveraged.

5.9.3. Importance of the Relationship

Not all relationships carry equal weight for the BRM. For the purposes of this exercise, we define four levels of importance of a relationship to the BRM:

1. Approver—this is the individual or group that approves major decisions concerning Provider investments or initiatives.

2. Decision Maker—this is the individual or group that makes major decisions concerning Provider investments or initiatives.

3. Evaluator—this is the individual or group that evaluates major decisions concerning Provider investments or initiatives.

4. User—this is the individual or group that uses the solutions enabled by the Provider investments or initiatives.

Once the Relationship Quality Diagnostic has been completed, the results should be plotted on the Relationship Value Map. The horizontal axis represents the Overall Quality of Relationship rating derived during this exercise. Qualitative factors may slightly adjust the score up (to the right) or down (to the left). The vertical axis represents the importance of the relationship. As a guide, the four roles used in the exercise are laid out along the vertical axis to illustrate that in general, approvers are more critical to the success of the relationship than decision makers, and so on. Key Executives falling in the *Improve* quadrant should have a relationship development plan created for them.

5.9.4. Application Notes

- The raw insights for the Relationship Value Map come from the Customer Value Hierarchy
- Both the content of the Value Hierarchy and the degree to which the expectations are satisfied should be validated with your Business Partner
- The vertical axis can be amended as needed for the situation
- If the sales language does not work, then other labels can be used (e.g. low-high influence)

5.10. Strategic Relationship Management

Strategic Relationship Management is used by BRMs and their teams to manage their key Business Partner relationships.

5.10.1. Background

While sales professionals responsible for external customers and clients invariably use some form of account management process, Business Relationship Managers responsible for internal Business Partner relationship typically do not. As such, their behaviors are often inconsistent and the Business Partner experience across a number of internal relationships are unpredictable. This page presents a Strategic Relationship Management Process appropriate for the types of strategic relationship for which the BRM is accountable.

5.10.2. Purpose

The Strategic Relationship Management Process should be customized for a given enterprise, but then followed consistently and diligently by both the BRM and their Business Partner Service Team. While the process is presented here as a linear series of stages, in practice these stages are often concurrent and iterative.

5.10.3. The BRM Business Partner Service Team

Throughout this Strategic Relationship Management Process, reference will be made to the Business Partner Service Team. Business Partner Service Teams have always existed in an informal way, are now much more important, given the complexity of the relationships that need to be managed. The BRM is not only responsible for managing relationships with the Business Partner (the demand side) but with the supply side as well. In fact, since they operate at the juncture of the two organizations, the BRM must simultaneously operate as the advocate of the customer (and appear so to the customer) and the representative of the IT organization (and appear so to the IT organization). The Business Partner Service Team typically consists of the BRM, who leads the team, as well as a Solution Delivery Manager (SDM), an IT Operations Manager (ITOM) and an Architect. This group should identify themselves as the Business Partner Service Team, and start to act in a coordinated and synchronized manner. Finally, it should be recognized that there is a team at work on the Business Partner's side as well. Rarely is it the case that the relationship is limited to the BRM and his or her counterpart. Instead, and as discussed below, the relationship almost always operates as a many-to-many model and not a one-to-one.

5.10.4. Strategic Relationship Management - Major Stages

Strategic Relationship Management illustrated in Figure 43 is a simple 5-stage approach to managing the relationships between a BRM and their Business Partners. Even though the stages are shown as sequential, in practice they occur simultaneously and continuously. For example, Discovery, rather than being a stage in a process, is an ongoing activity. Similarly, Planning and Execution represent core competencies that are constantly refreshed. Each of these stages is described in greater detail in the sections that follow.

5.10.5. Stage 1 - Initiation/Overview

The first stage in the process is to assemble the Business Partner Service Team with the membership suggested above. The members of the team will likely have been working independently on behalf of the Business Partner, with different sources and types of information, different relationship strategies, different relationships and different outcomes. There is likely to have been little formal organization and no coordinated roles and responsibilities. Thus, this stage in the process focuses on team formation and organization, and on creating a coherent, coordinated approach to serving the client. Without this level of planning, the likelihood of moving beyond an ad hoc relationship is low indeed.

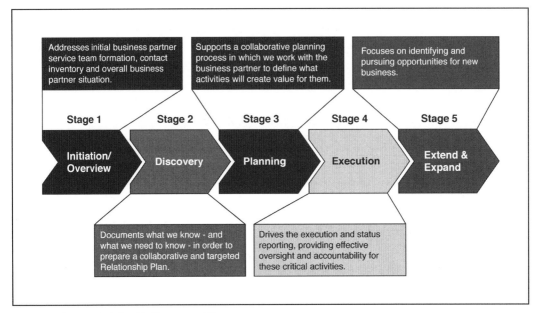

Figure 43 - Strategic Relationship Management Stages

There are four specific tasks that may need to be addressed as part of the Initiation/Overview stage.

Task 1: Contact Inventory

Business Partner relationships are rarely one-to-one, but instead operate in a many-to-many model as the aggregation of multiple one-to-one relationships. In this case, the relationship of the BRM with his or her direct contact represents the tip of the iceberg on both sides. Below each of the primary players is an organization of people who are working on a daily basis with contacts on the other team. The lack of alignment and coordination of these one-to-one relationships causes miscommunication of expectations, commitments, understanding and objectives. Therefore it is imperative that the BRM, as the Business Partner Service Team leader, create an inventory of the multiple one-to-one relationships that need to be coordinated and aligned within the context of the overall relationship.

Task 2: Synthesize Information & Knowledge

Knowledge about the Business Partner is rarely managed as a central asset. It will be necessary to collect what is known about the customer and their business objectives, and make sure that the knowledge is available to all team members. This activity will inform the Discover effort in Stage 2, and will help avoid the frustration that the customer experiences when he or she has to explain something over and over again.

It can be highly beneficial to use some type of Customer Relationship Management tool that can be shared by the Business Partner Service Team and other IT stockholders. If the firm is already using a tool such as Salesforce. com, that can be a good choice.

Task 3: Team Organization and Roles

The creation of intentional Business Partner Service Teams will be a new activity for many team members (as well as many Business Partners). Time should be spent on making sure that each team member knows what their role is, and the expectations that the BRM and the Business Partner have of and for them.

Task 4: Skill Development and Training

Finally, the BRM should use the time together with the Business Partner Service Team to make sure that critical Relationship management competencies are communicated, and that team members are able to discharge the duties to which they have been assigned. These competencies may include things such as active listening, dealing with objections/complaints, interviewing skills, presentation skills, reporting and others.

5.10.6. Stage 2 - Discovery

The most common problem that afflicts Business Partner Service Teams is that they assume that what they know is all they need to know. In many, if not most cases, the limitations that exist in their relationships with their Business Partners result from an incomplete understanding of the Business Partner's needs, priorities and value expectations. In fact, if the team does not actively determine what it needs to know, and then fill those knowledge gaps, it is unlikely that the outcome will improve. The closing of the knowledge gap regarding the Business Partner's needs is addressed in this Discovery stage using the Customer Value Hierarchy, which is described in the Tools and Templates section.

Conducting Discovery Interviews

There are several benefits to taking the Discovery task seriously and investing time and effort in the process. First and foremost is the fact that there are few activities that are as effective in building trust and confidence as simply asking "What is important to you?" Even thinking carefully about that question, and validating the conclusions with the Business Partner is useful.

A second benefit is the fact that the outcome becomes sort of a contract with the Business Partner—you have agreed with them on what is important, and can confidently prioritize accordingly. Note that this will also limit the likelihood that the team might over-invest in Got-to-Have Expectations (see Customer Value Hierarchy tool), wasting time, effort and money.

The information itself is often useful in making sure that the Business Partner Service Team is "on the same page." In many cases, teams disagree about what is most important to the customer, which is reflected in uncoordinated team activities and siloed behavior. (This alignment is often as useful on the Business Partner side as it is for the Business Partner Service Team.)

The only way to complete discovery and close the knowledge gap is to talk to your Business Partner. Each of us enters the partnership with preconceived notions, assumptions and perspectives that act as filters when we look at our Business Partner's business. This means that the most serious mistake that can be made in this process is to assume that one already knows what is important to one's customer. That assumption, in and of itself, is virtually guaranteed to create a knowledge gap!

Discovery Interview Guidelines

Conducting Discovery interviews is more common with external customers than with internal Business Partners. When speaking with external customers, sales and Relationship management professionals draw on a library of open-ended questions that are useful in getting customers to articulate their higher order value expectations. These questions may be useful to BRM's in planning and conducting Discovery interviews with internal customers:

1. Think about your best internal or external Business Partners—your "*A" relationships*. What is it about those relationships that really makes a difference to your operation?

2. I believe we are generally meeting the terms of our SLA/contract (obviously, don't assert that if it is not clearly true!) What else should we be focusing on to improve performance?

3. What other things do we need to pay attention to? How are we doing in those areas now?

4. Of all the people in your organization who follow our performance or know about our work here, who has the least favorable impression? Why is that? What could we do to improve that?

5. We'd like to be so highly regarded here that you would refer us to your colleagues in other parts of the business. Is there anything that would prevent you from doing that now?

6. What is the next IT opportunity that we should be thinking about here? What do we need to do in order to get started on that opportunity?

7. Where do you see your next position in the company? What do you need to accomplish in order to achieve that objective?

5.10.7. Stage 3 - Planning

The most effective customer and Business Partner relationships are those in which both parties play an active role in planning how the relationship will operate. In cases where relationship planning is done for (or, even worse, to) the customer, they may feel disconnected and a lack of ownership from the resulting plan.

Within the context of this Framework, this planning activity focuses on the relationship and not on technology. Put another way, the Technology Roadmap that is required of each BRM and each Business Partner should address what work is being done. The relationship planning activity describes how that work will be done.

The reason for the distinction between the technology roadmap and the relationship planning activity (and the emphasis on the latter) is simple. Research has shown that when customer relationships underperform, the most common reason is that while the parties were clear on what needed to be done, the question of how they would work together was rarely asked and even more rarely answered.

A second critical consideration is that problems that are bilateral in nature can rarely be solved unilaterally. Most performance-limiting problems in Business Partner relationships are not caused exclusively by one party or the other. In fact, it is often the case that one party is blissfully unaware of the unintended consequences of their actions, and the fact that they are perhaps contributing to the very performance problems about which they complain most bitterly. In cases such as this, a bilateral and collaborative approach to relationship problem solving must be used. Put simply, the Business Partner Service Team can only solve problems for which they are exclusively responsible—all others must be addressed together.

The tool that we use to support this collaborative planning activity is the Relationship Strategy on a Page. The structure is illustrated in Figure 44, and discussed in more detail in the Techniques section under Building a Relationship Strategy on a Page. What is most important to remember about the Relationship Strategy on a Page is that it is not the template that creates value, but the process of completing the template. Working through the content of each of the sections, particularly if it is done in a facilitated process, will surface important questions and issues. These issues, when addressed and resolved, will allow the relationship to operate at a higher level of effectiveness and efficiency.

The Planning activity typically follows Discovery. In fact, if Discovery is done well (that is, if the Knowing Gap is smaller), then planning can focus on creating breakthrough value instead of better sameness. It should also be mentioned that the Relationship Strategy on a Page should focus on the relationship and not a project. The relationship should transcend individual projects, and provide a foundation for effective execution of discrete pieces of work, but should operate at a higher level of strategy and alignment.

5.10.8. Stage 4 - Execution

Once the Business Partner Service Team is aligned, discovery activities have been completed, and you have collaborated with the customer in the development of a relationship strategy, execution is simply a matter of doing what has been agreed upon. Ideally, the set of tasks outlined in the Relationship Strategy on a Page will focus on the key relationship capabilities needed to transform the relationship from an efficient order-taking mode to a strategic partnership (see the Business Relationship Maturity Framework).

Typically, efficient project execution is more of a core competency and more likely to be present than either Discovery and Planning. Accordingly, this is the stage that is likely to be most robust. The greater risk is that we will simply skip Planning and Discovery, and jump directly into Execution, since we are more comfortable with the latter, and the former stages may be unnatural acts. Keep in mind that doing so limits the Business Partner outcome to Better Sameness, and fails to address the systemic relationship issues that have and will continue to limit the value created by the partnership.

5.10.9. Stage 5 - Extension and Expansion

Extension and expansion have different meanings for internal relationships than for commercial relationships or relationships with external stakeholders. When dealing with external customers, one is concerned about financial or scope expansion, measured in terms of revenue, additional projects or customer loyalty. For other types of external stakeholders (members, donors, supporters, students, etc.), expansion may mean a broader relationship, higher levels of giving, greater loyalty or deeper involvement and time commitment. Internally, the meaning focuses more on maintenance and relationship maturity.

Traditionally, relationship management plans were done in order to fulfill an administrative requirement, and were not used or consulted until the next planning cycle. They were prepared unilaterally, often not even shown to the customer and were generally viewed as an administrative exercise. Within IT, however, our intent is different. Not only is the planning meant to target the most important performance issues, but the resulting Relationship Strategy on a Page and relationship plan is meant to provide day-to-day guidance for both the Business Partner and the Business Partner Service Team. Therefore, it is essential that the documents be kept up to date and current.

Specifically, maintenance of the process means three things.

1. The Customer Value Hierarchy should be revisited on a regular basis. We suggest that this be done quarterly at first, adjusting the frequency according to the rate at which the customer's needs and value expectations change.

2. As the Key Initiatives are accomplished, new initiatives should be defined and incorporated into the Relationship Strategy on a Page.

3. The overall strategy will evolve, and the Relationship Strategy on a Page should be maintained accordingly.

Extension and expansion in terms of relationship maturity involves moving from an order taker role to more of a strategic partner. The evolution within an individual relationship is hard to measure objectively, but each BRM should be alert to opportunities to contribute at a higher, more strategic level.

Having said that, the Business Partner gets to decide on the kind of relationship they wish to have with their BRM and the extended Business Partner Service Team. Even though the BRM aspires to be a strategic partner, he or she cannot force a Business Partner into that kind of relationship. There are two ways to encourage the development of more of a strategic relationship.

1. The first way is illustrated using the Business Relationship Management Maturity Framework. Order Taker relationships tend to be highly transactional and focus primarily on the lifecycle stage entitled "Acquire New Execution Capability." BRMs who wish to transform their relationship should make a conscious effort to stay engaged with the Business Partner after the transaction, and seek to create value in the latter two lifecycle stages, "Implement and Operationalize" and "Operate and Improve Performance."

2. The second key to moving the relationship to a more strategic level is to focus intentionally on the Discovery and Planning stages in the Strategic Relationship Management Process. BRM's should resist the temptation to move directly to the Execution Stage. Moving directly to Execution, more than anything else, will reinforce a transactional kind of relationship in which the role of the BRM is to execute against plans and agendas to which they have not had a chance to contribute.

5.11. Repairing Broken Business Partner Relationships

Techniques for Repairing Broken Relationships between a Provider and their Business Partner.

5.11.1. Background

BRMs often find themselves stepping into or inheriting broken relationships between a Provider and their Business Partner.

5.11.2. Situation 1: Poor Provider Performance

- Gather data about Provider performance and trends
- Discuss data-gathering results with Business Partner
- Develop performance metrics and standards
- Monitor behavior and publish results

5.11.3. Situation 2: Lack of Trust from Business Partner Due To Prior Bad Provider Experience

- But they may not tell you that—can be difficult to diagnose
- Can't resolve by saying "it wasn't me"
- Can't resolve by improving technical performance
- Must build the relationship—start small, have positive interactions; give help and jargon-free information; locate near clients and see them often

5.11.4. Finding Allies and Other Political Maneuvers

Politics means trying to advance a change agenda. Change is essential to getting value from Provider investments, otherwise why invest in them? The Provider must often advance change agendas without mandating change, therefore they must find allies (use political analysis) and convince stakeholders to act. The best allies are not necessarily the line units—other staff units often have great leverage on line units. For example, accounting/finance can frequently be a particularly useful ally.

5.12. Building the Relationship Strategy on a Page

The Relationship Strategy on a Page (RSOAP) is used by BRMs and their Account Teams. As with Building a Customer Value Hierarchy, the value in this technique is the process of completing it rather than the completed form itself. In this page, we describe the content and structure of the RSOAP, and suggest an approach for completing it.

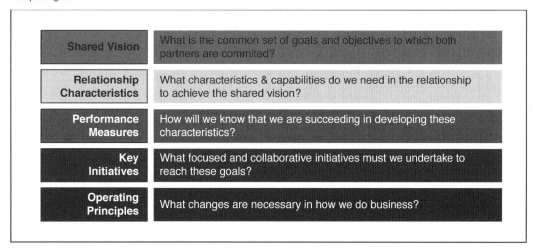

Shared Vision	What is the common set of goals and objectives to which both partners are commited?
Relationship Characteristics	What characteristics & capabilities do we need in the relationship to achieve the shared vision?
Performance Measures	How will we know that we are succeeding in developing these characteristics?
Key Initiatives	What focused and collaborative initiatives must we undertake to reach these goals?
Operating Principles	What changes are necessary in how we do business?

Figure 44 - Relationship Strategy on a Page

5.12.1. Background

The Relationship Strategy on a Page is a variation on the *Strategy on a Page*, but addresses the strategy a BRM will create for developing the relationship with his or her Business Partner.

5.12.2. Purpose

The Relationship Strategy on a Page should be developed jointly between the BRM (or the Account Team) and the Business Partner. It is an output of the Strategic Relationship Management process.

5.12.3. Contracting with Your Business Partner

In many ways, mutually developing and agreeing to a Relationship Strategy On a Page is a powerful mechanism for contracting between the BRM and their Business Partner. It involves working through a process to reach a mutual understanding of results to be achieved and means to achieve them. Contracting clarifies commitments and expectations of both parties, laying out a road map of activities and initiatives that collectively achieve the targeted results.

5.12.4. Structure

The RSOAP consists of five sections which are completed in a top down fashion collaboratively with the Business Partner, preferably in a facilitated workshop setting involving the affected teams of people on both sides. As we

discuss the sections, it is important to keep in mind that each section (from the top down) informs the one below it.

Shared Vision

The RSOAP starts with the articulation of a Shared Vision for the Relationship. This should not be the vision of one party or the other, but should be a stretch goal that requires (and is impossible to achieve without) active participation and investment from both parties. A robust statement of shared vision has the following characteristics:

- It is concrete, and describes a future state that is both realistic and real. BRM's should avoid statements of shared vision that are abstract, figurative and which are hard to understand. One good way to test the concreteness of the vision statement is to ask whether or not we'd know it if we achieved it!

- It is value-based. The shared vision should represent an objective that is highly attractive and represents real value for both parties.

- It is balanced in the sense that it represents proportional value and investment for both parties. Vision statements which are attractive to only one part fail the test for balance.

- It is jointly owned. Joint ownership means that pursuing the vision requires collaboration between the parties, both in terms of the investment of time and money, but also in terms of actively working together.

- It is ambitious, and represents a stretch goal that would not be achieved without the active collaboration of both parties. It should test and reflect the kind of collaboration to which the relationship aspires.

Creating a Shared Vision Between the Business Partner Team and Provider Account Team

There are several ways in which to generate a shared vision. One of the most popular is to have each team (e.g. the Business Partner team and the Account Team) brainstorm the nature of the future state that would be most attractive to the other team. Each team, role-playing as the other side in the relationship, should think about the outcomes that would be most satisfying and most ambitious. To accomplish this in a workshop environment, divide attendees into two teams, one from the Business Partner and one from the Provider organization. After having provided background and context, the Business Partner team should brainstorm on the following question from the point of view of the IT account team, and the account team should brainstorm as though they were the Business Partner team:

Instructions to the Business Partner Team:

Imagine that you returned to the Provider Account Team after an absence of 18-24 months. Your colleagues on the team were excited to share with you how the relationship with the business unit had grown and matured, and where it stood today. After they had finished showing you and telling you about the remarkable progress that had been made, you were astonished. You never thought that this much progress was possible in such a short period of time, or that things could be as good as they were currently. Later that afternoon, you reflected on your colleagues' excitement and enthusiasm, and started to make some notes about what you had seen and heard.

What did you write down?

Instructions to the IT Account Team:

Imagine that you returned to this business unit after an absence of 18-24 months. Your colleagues in the business unit were excited to share with you how the relationship with the Provider had grown and matured and where it stood today. After they had finished showing you and telling you about the remarkable progress that had been made, you were astonished. You never thought that this much progress was possible in such a short period of time, or that things could be as good as they were currently. Later that afternoon, you reflected on your colleagues' excitement and enthusiasm, and started to make some notes on what you had seen and heard.

What did you write down?

Creating Shared Vision - Team Instructions

At least 45 minutes should be allowed for the exercise. The teams should be instructed to make notes that are as descriptive and detailed as they can be, to be ambitious (even a little unrealistic), and to not worry about how they would get there. The point is to create an outcomes statement—A Shared Vision—that is rich in detail and equally compelling to both parties. After the teams have done their brainstorming, they should reconvene as a single group, compare notes, and do the following:

Each team should share the work that was done, articulating the vision that they brainstormed for and on behalf of the other team. During this report out, special attention should be paid to the assumptions that are implicit in the work that was done, and whether those assumptions are accurate.

Clarify the individual team visions so that the Business Partner team agrees with the work done on their behalf and the account team agrees with the work done on their behalf.

Converge the visions into a single integrated vision, paying close attention to the words that are used and to the meaning associated with those words. In the example of a completed RSOAP which reflects the work done by two teams over 12 hours of work, many of the words were discussed and the meanings refined significantly. Words such as "partnership," "collaboration," "mutual," and "risk" all had deep meaning for these two teams.

Given the complexity and depth of meaning, it is easy to over invest in the statement of shared vision. In practice, it is usually sufficient to get to the 80% level of completion, since the process of working through the other four parts of the RSOAP will raise questions about the vision, and will refine what was meant (or not meant) by one team or the other.

The outcome should be an ambitious outcomes statement that is attractive and aspirational for both parties in the relationship, and which cannot be achieved except via the collaboration of the parties. If the Shared Vision is only meaningful to one party, the exercise has failed to achieve its most basic goal.

5.12.5. Relationship Characteristics

Inevitably, one common reaction to the Shared Vision will be that it is unrealistic and naïve to think that the parties could achieve it. This skepticism arises out of the fact that the relationship, as currently constituted and as it currently operates, could never support as lofty and ambitious a goal. The next section of the RSOAP, then, asks the question "What are the characteristics and capabilities that we need in this working relationship in order to achieve this goal which now seems unattainable?"

Relationship Characteristics

In general, the capabilities refer to things that the parties are able to do within the context of the relationship, such as create value, or collaborate or innovate. The characteristics refer to nature of the relationship – whether it is transparent, trust-based, growth-oriented, etc. BRMs and Account Teams should be very careful not to defer to this list, but to be alert to other characteristics and capabilities which are not listed.

The best source of insight for identifying the missing or incomplete characteristics and capabilities is the preceding discussion on the Shared Vision. In the course of that discussion, comments, observations, doubts and skepticism will be expressed – each of these, in a very concrete way, reflects the absence of a critical characteristic or capability. And of course, the absence of a characteristic or a capability may be expressed as the presence of an obstacle.

In this case, the teams identified the absence of trust and transparency, communication and the lack of coordination between Provider supply and demand as key obstacles that needed to be overcome.

Relationship Characteristics that May be Missing	Relationship Capabilities that May be Missing
· Transparency	· Value Creation
· Trust	· Collaboration
· Confidence	· Roadmap Alignment/ Involvement
· Security	· Agility & Flexibility
· Shared Risk/Return	· Predictability
· Referenceability	· Communication
· Growth	· Innovation
· Others?	· Others?

5.12.6. Performance Measures

The order of the next two sections is very important. It is common for the Performance Measures to follow, not precede, the identification of Key Initiatives. In the RSOAP, the order is inverted. The primary reason for this is that when teams focus first on what they choose to do, and then on the measures by which their progress will be evaluated, they tend to be limited by the status quo and existing constraints. Initiatives often bear a striking similarity to work that has already been commissioned and may already be underway, but these pre-existing projects often are completely unaligned with either the Shared Vision or the Relationship Characteristics.

The questions that one asks are very different depending on the order in which these next two sections are addressed. When one identifies the Key Initiatives first, the question being asked is "What do we get if we do this work?" When one identifies the Performance Measures first, the question is "What do we need to do in order to achieve this outcome?" We are committed to the second, outcomes-based approach.

The most challenging aspect of defining the performance measures is to create meaningful quantitative measures for qualitative outcomes. Obviously, outcomes such as trust and transparency are exceptionally difficult to measure, not only because they are abstract, but also because they are highly subjective in nature.

The first approach is to measure an activity which is a precursor to the outcome of interest. For example, the measure of "60 minute email notifications for all SLA exceptions" does not measure trust and transparency directly, but measures an activity which both parties recognized was critical to the development of trust and transparency.

The second approach is to measure the consequences of failing to address the outcome of interest. In the example, we can see that the teams recognized that their inability to coordinate demand and supply was a key obstacle in achieving the Shared Vision. Measuring coordination is somewhat of an abstraction, so measures were defined that evaluated the consequences of failure, namely the need to bring in supplementary labor in addition to the resources for which the Business Partner had already contracted.

One final note on Performance Measures. There exists a bias against qualitative measures in some organizations, as though they were "softer," less concrete or somehow less reliable as a basis for decision making. However, when one investigates underperforming working relationships, the reason is almost always found in these qualitative characteristics. Organizations tend to have better tools and processes for managing facts than feelings, but it is the feelings that are often most performance-limiting.

5.12.7. Key Initiatives

The Key Initiatives are those actions, which, in the short term, are needed to start to make progress toward the Shared Vision. These initiatives are **not** simply a listing of the projects that are underway, for two reasons. The existing projects almost never have very much to do with how the relationship is working or how value is being created. More often, they focus on the transactions and the technology content of the relationship. In addition, the existing projects, since they were defined prior to the work on the RSOAP, will tend to reinforce the status quo, and not the new relationship that we are trying to create with our customers.

The initiatives should exist in support of the previous sections of the RSOAP. These are the specific short term actions which are necessary to develop the relationship characteristics that are needed in order to achieve the Shared Vision. Each definition should launch a team, staffed by members of the Account Team and the Business Partner team, who will work on the named project and be held accountable according to the Performance Measures that have been defined.

In addition to not simply regurgitating a list of existing projects, there are several other criteria which should be kept in mind when defining the Key Initiatives.

- They should be projects that require the collaboration of both parties. Note that this is not a very restrictive criteria, since the only problems that do NOT require the involvement of both parties are those which have been exclusively caused by the account team. And despite the claims to the contrary, both parties contribute to virtually every relationship problem.

- They should be projects from which both parties will benefit. Collaboration is difficult when the value accrues to only one party.

- They should be problems that have historically been difficult to solve unilaterally. Many problems in relationships have been there for a while, during which one party or the other (most often the account team!) has been blamed and has tried to solve it alone.

- At the beginning, BRMs should seek to define initiatives which are smaller and more tractable. This will make the collaborative approach a little easier, and hopefully create some quick wins.

Key Initiatives, after they have been defined, will need to be described more fully in order to get funding or authorization to proceed. Project planning can be done many ways, but a simple template is provided in the Appendix. Following this modest project planning step, it will be necessary to get the go-ahead from executives on both sides of the relationship, particularly if the investment of time and money is needed.

Finally, when deciding on which initiatives should be selected, some guidelines may help:

- Given the highly aspirational nature of the Shared Vision, it will be easy to bite off more than the Business Partner and account teams can chew.

- First things first. In some cases, the path toward developing the necessary relationship characteristics and capabilities is a long one. The initiatives should be focused on taking the necessary next step, and not skipping over important milestones.

- Objectives and scope should be concrete, and the resource requirements should be reasonable. Underfunding the teams working on the initiatives is the best way to limit their chances of success, and communicate that the work is not valued.

Finally and perhaps most importantly, the focus on Key Initiatives must be on those things that need to be done this quarter, not next year. The RSOAP should describe what the teams need to be working on NOW in order to create success in the future.

In the completed RSOAP, the teams identified specific actions that were needed in order to satisfy the Performance Measures. In order to satisfy the measures under "Greater Degree of Openness, Transparency and Trust," for example, the teams decided to establish a Communications Task Force and to initiate a daily email bulletin. The initiatives undertaken in support of "Coordination of Supply and Demand Between the Partners" included efforts directed at demand predictability. Obviously, none of these descriptions is sufficient to understand specifically what will be done, by whom or how, which is described in a separate project plan, but they do represent the commitment of the parties to try and address the factors which limit the productivity and success of the relationship.

5.12.8. Operating Principles

The last section in the RSOAP is where we make the changes in the way we operate the relationship explicit. Without some change in our operating principles, it is almost certain that the relationship will revert back to its old state, with its attendant performance problems and frustrations.

Good principles take a stand between two valid alternatives (as opposed to support for the only principle that makes any sense at all). It is in this section where the account team can address ways of operating that will help make the changes in the relationship sustainable.

Examples of new operating principles for internal relationships might include:

- The level of funding for an internal project shall not be less than the price submitted by the lowest qualified external bidder.

- Ongoing performance data shall be maintained so that it can be accessed by the Business Partner, and will be reviewed only briefly at QBR meetings.

- We agree to an annual offsite meeting to be hosted by the Provider at which we will discuss the strategy plans for the business and the implications for the Provider.

- Selection of technology is to be done by the Provider in accordance with corporate processes. The BU recognizes that maintenance of multiple technologies is neither feasible nor useful.

In each case, it is possible to see that the principle makes a specific choice between two valid options. The consequence of each statement is that employees will have to stop doing some things and start doing others. The Operating Principles are oriented more to a relationship with an external customer, but still illustrate how they were used to "put a stake in the ground" around a contentious issue or topic. As such, they are illustrative of the process for our application to internal relationships.

5.13. Building a Relationship Improvement Plan

The Relationship Improvement Plan is typically used after Building a Customer Value Hierarchy and Diagnosing Relationship Quality techniques have been used as part of the Strategic Relationship Management process.

5.13.1. Background

The Relationship Improvement Plan technique is an approach to planning the improvement of the Business-Provider working relationship for the purposes of driving higher business value from Provider investments and assets.

5.13.2. Purpose

The Relationship Improvement Plan is an output of the Strategic Relationship Management process, used to document the approach that will be taken to strengthen the relationship with key business executives.

5.13.3. Relationship Improvement Plan

After Building a Customer Value Hierarchy and Diagnosing Relationship Quality, the Relationship Improvement Plan should be completed.

Key Executive Relationship Improvement Plan					
Contact Name / Title		**Rel. Strength**	Weak	**Rel. Importance**	High
Primary / Secondary Contacts					
What value expectations remain unmet (from the Client Value Hierarchy)					
What other challenges exist in the relationship?					
What is the strategy for improving the relationship?					
Executive Contact					
Communication					
Special Initiatives					
Other					

5.13.4. Application Notes

The Relationship Improvement Plan is one way to record the specific actions for addressing the identified weaknesses

It should refer back to the Customer Value Hierarchy for specific needs that are not being addressed

The Relationship Improvement Plan is typically not shared with your Business Partner, although there is no reason why it could not be collaboratively shared and implemented

Business Relationship Management Institute

Page Intentionally Left Blank

6. Competencies

6.1. Business Transition Management

Business Transition Management (BTM) is a deliberate approach for managing the human dynamics before, during and after implementing a business change initiative in order to prevent *business value leakage*.

6.1.1. Background

Business Transition Management ensures that business areas impacted by an initiative are identified, understand and are prepared for the business transition (not just the technology transition) so that disruption to business operations is minimized and the full value of the project is achieved.

We use the term 'Business Transition Management' because this term puts the focus on the transition your business partners must make to achieve the full value of an initiative. Though the core work within Business Transition Management is often referred to as *Organizational Change Management (OCM)*, OCM is a term that gets used in many other ways within an organization, and also, at times, gets confused with the ITIL term *IT Change Management*.

6.1.2. Purpose

BTM identifies shifts (beyond the technology shifts) required for a successful initiative:

- Processes
- Behaviors and Mindsets
- Language/Terminology
- Roles, Structure, Reporting Relationships
- Teaming Interactions
- Culture
- Day-to-Day Operations
- Physical Locations

BTM identifies who is impacted by a business transition and the network of sponsors, change agents and advocates needed to make the changes happen. BTM paves the way for strong and sustained sponsorship, engages stakeholders, creates buy-in, and prepares individuals and groups by determining who should be engaged and how (e.g. communication, involvement in design, training, etc.). Finally, BTM helps your Business Partners plan their *readiness activities* for a smooth cutover when the initiative is implemented, and ongoing business operations.

Doing these things helps ensure you harvest the full value you anticipated from the initiative being implemented.

6.1.3. The Role of BRM in Business Transition Management

BTM is important to the BRM for two reasons:

- In the BRM role as Transition Advisor to Business Partners, to ensure that business transitions related to Portfolio Initiatives go smoothly so that they are successful and enable the full business value to be harvested.
- In the BRM role as Transition Leader in the implementation of a BRM role, to ensure smooth adoption of the BRM role; that the BRM role works effectively with other key Provider and Business Partner roles, and to ensure that business demand is effectively shaped and that Provider supply is well coordinated to enable the highest value from the Provider investment portfolio.

As a BRM, you need not be a Business Transition Management or OCM expert!

- You need sufficient BTM skills to help your Business Partners and Provider partners be successful.
- You need to know when and how to engage skilled BTM/OCM specialists.

As a BRM, you should be advising your Business Partner to help ensure Business Transition Management happens to fully harness Business Value!

- Educating your Business Partner on the BTM activities and the value of doing each
- Knowing which BTM activities are critical
- Alerting your Business Partner of BTM risk areas
- Identifying areas in need of BTM/OCM expertise and partnering with BTM/OCM specialist teams

6.2. Myths and the realities of Business Transition Management (BTM).

6.2.1. Background

Those leading major business transitions often approach change with a conviction about the need to change and a clear vision of results of the change. To them, it is blindingly obvious that the change is absolutely essential, that there is a future state that will be infinitely superior to the current state, and that the change will be relatively straightforward. The realities, and the view by those expected to change their knowledge, skills, processes or behaviors is usually quite different!

6.2.2. The Myth of Change

People often use the terms "Current State" and "Future State" to describe the current situation they are trying to remedy and the new situation they are trying to create. The "Myth of Change," defines the typical hope that the journey from Current to Future state will be simple and compelling—once people have been presented with an idea of what the Future State will look like, and how it will alleviate problems in the Current State, they will naturally and enthusiastically migrate to the Future State. The reality, of course, is very different.

6.2.3. Unlocking the Organizational Immune System

In practice, transition occurs only when certain conditions apply, as expressed in a formula for change originally created by Richard Beckhard and David Gleicher, then refined by Kathie Dannemiller and sometimes called Gleicher's Formula. This formula provides a model to assess the relative strengths affecting the likely success or otherwise of the launch of organizational change programs.

$$(U \times V \times FS) > R$$

Three factors must be present for the launch of a meaningful organizational change to take place. These factors are:

- U = Urgency for the change based upon dissatisfaction with how things are now
- V = Vision of what is possible
- FS = First, concrete steps that can be taken towards the vision

If the product of these three factors is greater than R (*Resistance*) then change is possible. Because U, V, and FS are multiplied, if any one is absent or low, then the product will be low and therefore not capable of overcoming the resistance. To ensure a successful change, it is necessary to use influence and strategic thinking in order to create vision and identify those crucial, early steps towards it. In addition, the organization must recognize and accept the dissatisfaction that exists by communicating industry trends, leadership ideas, best practice and competitive analysis to identify the necessity for change.

6.2.4. How Pain Drives Change

Figure 45 illustrates four common ways that *pain* drives change. Unfortunately, the strongest motivator of change tends to be a current problem! Successful change leaders generate a sense of current problem long before the need is desperate—they are able to translate the failure to grasp a future opportunity in terms of current pain.

Pain is generally insufficient to drive change. To drive major change, people need to understand and believe in:

- The Pain. Why the current state is untenable. What unwanted conditions exist today or will exist in the future? What opportunities are we unable to take advantage of today, or will not be available to us in the future?

- The Remedy. How will the future state address the current state issues? How compelling is the vision? The remedy should be communicated with a strong element of "What's In It For Me?" (WIIFM) i.e. the remedy (and the pain!) should be audience-specific!

- The Path. How will we get from the current to future state? Again, this needs to be communicated with a strong WIIFM (i.e. audience-specific!)

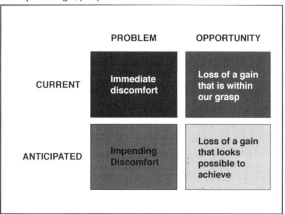

Figure 45 - Pain and Opportunity Grid

The successful transition leader is diligent about and skilled in communicating the pain, the remedy to that pain and the path to a future state that addresses the pain.

6.3. Business Transition Management Capability Model

A Business Transition Management Capability Model describes the key Capabilities necessary to clarify, motivate, orchestrate, drive, sustain and monitor major business transition.

6.3.1. Background

Successful business transition demands a set of capabilities to move the change from concept to reality.

Figure 46 illustrates a Framework for the BRMI Provider Capability Model for Business Transition Management.

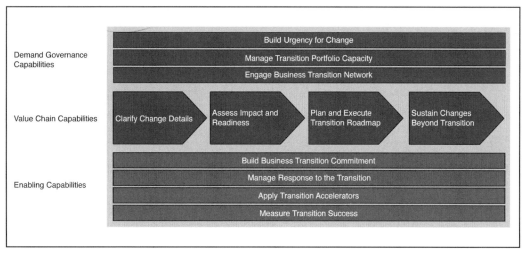

Figure 46 - BTM Capability Model

6.3.2. Build Urgency for Change

(© 2003 Omega Point Consulting, L.L.C. – reprinted with permission)

This helps answer the question: "Why Change?" Urgency for change is often built around the business drivers, and typically include:

- Strategic issues (e.g. our business strategy depends upon making this change)
- Financial issues (e.g. we can no longer afford to have so many redundant platforms)
- Customer issues (e.g. we need to deliver a seamless, superb customer experience, but our current, silo'd mode of working does not allow that)
- Operational issues (e.g. our current processes are too error prone and lead to excessive waste)
- Employee-related issues (e.g. employee engagement is low and getting worse, which is impacting our ability to compete)
- Regulatory issues (e.g. the industry regulations mandate that we adopt this change by the end of the year)
- Social issues (e.g. our *green footprint* is becoming a factor that limits our growth in our key markets)

What is critical is to take the business drivers from the business case and translate them into specific pain or remedy targeted to the audiences being asked to change; use the current/future problem/opportunity matrix to drive the details as though you were having a conversation with a target audience.

As Figure 45, "Pain and Opportunity Grid" illustrated, urgency can be created from both problems (current and anticipated) and opportunities that may be lost (current and anticipated). To create urgency at all Levels in the organization, convert business drivers into what people care about, and use their language! Frame the problem or opportunity in a way that resonates with a specific problem or opportunity of theirs.

6.3.3. Manage Transition Portfolio Capacity

Middle management is often pressured by senior executives to make change happen, while concurrently facing resistance from first line managers and staff. Additionally, their current performance management mechanisms tend to reinforce the current state. This makes the role of change leader by middle management a very difficult one. An important aspect of empowering these change leaders at the middle management level is to form them into a supportive network to help each other deal with the transition issues and leverage opportunities to move the changes forward. It is also important to recognize that these change leaders at the middle cannot make the transition happen on their own. They need the help of a broader network of individuals who play specific roles in managing the change dynamics and moving the transition forward.

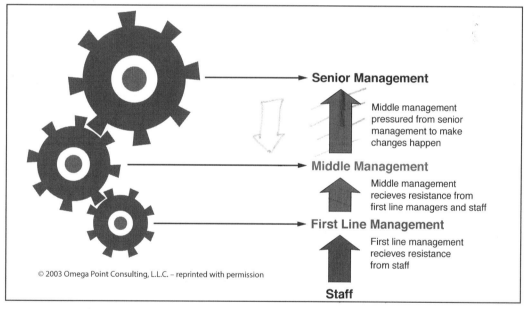

© 2003 Omega Point Consulting, L.L.C. – reprinted with permission

Figure 47 - Middle Management Capacity for Change Is Often the Limiting Factor

6.3.4. Engage Business Transition Network

The Transition Network is the key to unlocking existing dynamics in the organization to move the change forward. It is helpful to think about the Transition Network as comprising five key roles necessary to orchestrate the change process:

- Stakeholders—Those Impacted in some way: they must change their knowledge, skills, processes, behaviors or mindsets

- Initiating Change Leader—The individual who Initiates, sponsors, and drives the change and validates the change for all Stakeholders

- Sustaining Change Leaders—Those who have local institutional power to Validate the change for others within their local organization

- Change Agents—Those who guide the Planning and Implementation of the change

- Advocates—Those who are not Initiating or Sustaining Change Leaders or Change Agents, but are needed to use their personal influence for the change

Typical Ineffective Change Leadership

A common situation—imagine a *town hall meeting* where the CIO announces to the entire IT organization that all proposed initiatives must now have a complete Business Case and be part of an overall Value Management process. Later that day the head of Strategy and Enterprise Architecture meets with her team and says, "Disregard what you heard about the Business Case need—we don't have time for that and the Business Partners will never go along with it!" What do you expect the people in the Strategy and Enterprise Architecture group to do? Correct, they ignore the Business Case directive. This situation is known as a *change management black hole*—there's an Initiating Change Leader (the CIO, in this case) but a lack of Sustaining Change Leadership (at least from Strategy and Enterprise Architecture).

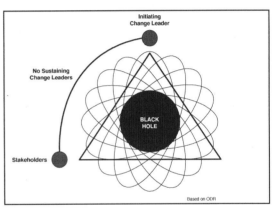

Figure 48 - The 'Black Hole' of Change

Black holes form when there is insufficient change leadership at the local levels closest to the people being asked to change. Sometimes this is because information about the change does not get passed along from one level of the organization to the next, or it does get passed along but not in a way that validates or supports the change. The *black hole* can form for various reasons, including:

- Unintentional confusion

- Covert sabotage

- Unwillingness for change leaders to challenge 'hiding places' of those being asked to change

- Lack of reinforcement of the change at the local levels

The core reason for the formation of *black holes* is lack of sustaining change leadership, reflecting a failure by the Initiating Change Leader to display the proper commitment to a change to those below them in the organization.

To prevent black holes, a full cascade of change leadership is necessary (see Figure 49). This will lay in place the local commitment and leadership of the change all the way down through the organization, and provide those who must change with solid direction about the change, and validation that it is a worthwhile effort.

Principles of Change Leadership

- Change Leadership is critical to successful change and cannot be delegated.
- Weak Change Leaders must be educated or replaced, or failure is inevitable.
- Initiating and Sustaining Change Leaders must never attempt to fulfill each other's role.
- Cascading Change Leadership must be established and maintained.

Cascading Change Leadership

(© 2003 Omega Point Consulting, L.L.C. – reprinted with permission)

Change Leadership is critical to successful change and cannot be delegated. Weak Change Leaders must be educated or replaced, or failure is inevitable. Initiating and Sustaining Change Leaders must never attempt to fulfill each other's role. Cascading Change Leadership must be established and maintained.

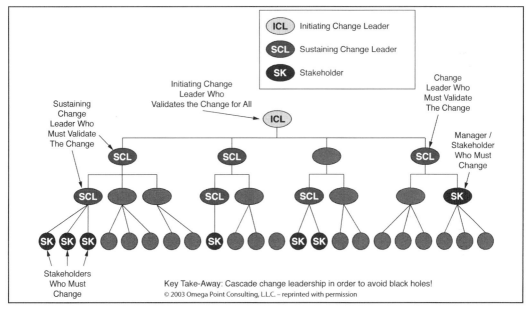

Figure 49 - Cascading Change Leadership

Assessing Support, Impact, and Influence

Once the Transition Network has been defined, an assessment of the individuals in the network in terms of their support for the change, their impact from the change, and their influence on others in the organization (i.e. "Are they opinion leaders?") will help identify where time and energy should be spent to gain stronger support or to leverage influence leaders.

Clarify the Change Details

(© 2003 Omega Point Consulting, L.L.C. – reprinted with permission)

It is important to clarify the change details so that people can see themselves in the future state. They need to be able to envision:

- Behaviors: how they will act differently
- Process: how they will work differently
- Relationships and Roles: how they will interact differently
- Mindset: how they will think differently
- Culture: what will be valued in the future
- Language: how they will talk differently
- Artifacts: what different things they will produce

There are numerous ways to drive to the details of the future state, including (but not limited to) the following:

- Create future state guiding principles
- Describe future state culture, behaviors, and mindsets
- Identify what's changing in From/To shifts
- Define what the future will look like, feel like, and sound like
- Create business process flows and other diagrams
- Describe a day in the life of a stakeholder in the future

It is also important to clarify the path to the future state, and again the *Cliff Metaphor* helps identify the types of approaches that can help clarify the path to change.

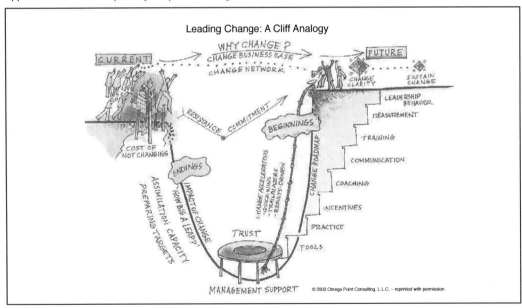

Figure 50 - Clarifying the Path to Change

6.3.5. Assess Impact and Change Readiness

(© 2003 Omega Point Consulting, L.L.C. – reprinted with permission)

This capability seeks to understand the impact of the business transition on all Stakeholders (see Figure 50) and the readiness of those Stakeholders and the broader organization to accept and adapt to the changes that will result from the transition. It is critical to understand the impact and readiness so that strategies can be developed to address the impacts and to improve the state of readiness, or adjust the change effort based on the state of readiness.

The capability draws upon the first Managing Business Transition Value Chain capability—Clarifying Change Details (see above). Given the changes to dimensions such as behaviors, processes, relationships, roles, mindset, culture, language, etc., impact and readiness assessment determines the breadth, depth and nature of impact, and the stakeholders readiness for those changes. Individuals and groups will likely be impacted at different levels for each of these dimensions. A proper assessment of impact should look at specific stakeholder groups as well as key individuals against these dimensions, and engage those groups and individuals in identifying the impacts, the magnitude of the changes, and what must be done to be 'ready' for the changes. By engaging stakeholders in the discussion, they gain a deeper understanding of the changes and are participating in creating the strategies to ensure they are ready for those changes. This helps build their commitment and surface key issues that may not have been anticipated by change leaders.

There are many ways to assess impact and readiness, including (but not limited to) the following:

- Facilitated sessions where groups of stakeholders (e.g. by department) discuss the future state (see Clarifying Change Details above), what is changing for them, and the steps that will be needed to be ready for those changes

- Completing surveys about typical change dimensions and readiness factors, and then analyzing those surveys to see patterns by stakeholder group, by change leaders, etc.

- Conversations with key individuals who have a good sense of the details of the future state and interviewing them deeply about the impacts to specific groups

- Researching similar organizations that have gone through similar changes to create a 'possible' list of likely changes and then using, facilitated sessions, or key conversations to validate which of those possible impacts will be true in your organization

The analysis of impact and readiness feeds the creation of strategies and plans for the transition (see the "Plan and Execute the Transition Roadmap" section).

6.3.6. Plan and Execute the Transition Roadmap

With the change details clarified and the impact and change readiness assessed, the next step is to create the roadmap that will be followed to guide the transition. There are many approaches and techniques for planning and executing a Transition Roadmap, depending upon the depth and scope of the change. A comprehensive Transition Roadmap will typically include sections on:

- Leadership Alignment
- Stakeholder Engagement and Commitment Building
- Transition Rollout and Acceptance
- Learning and Development
- Communications and Collaboration
- Business Transition Management Coordination
- Sustaining the Change

6.3.7. Sustain Changes Beyond the Transition

Sustaining change is a true test of leadership. It requires the use of a unique set of principles different from those used to initiate change. The incredibly strong gravity pull of old habits begins the moment a change has been made. Initiating a change is started using external energy–the energy of creating urgency through dissatisfaction with the current state, a burning platform or other urgency building mechanisms. Sustaining a change requires internal energy within the organization as people live the change, and talk about it. It also requires reinforcement, which is the glue to hold the change. Reinforcement can take a number of forms, including the following:

- Rewards & recognition
- Clear roles in the future state
- Cultural changes that reinforce the new ways
- Leadership behaviors, walking the talk
- Use of the new language

6.3.8. Build Business Transition Commitment

Different types of change require different levels of commitment that in turn demand different types and levels of communication.

Because change often manifests itself as a disruption to expectations, it affects the *6 Cs*:

- Control
- Competence
- Consistency
- Comfort
- Confidence
- Commitment

This disruption of expectations and impact on a sense of control, competence, etc. causes emotional responses to the change.

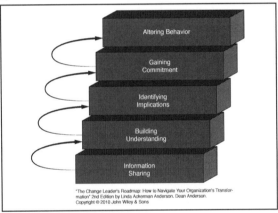

"The Change Leader's Roadmap: How to Navigate Your Organization's Transformation" 2nd Edition by Linda Ackerman Anderson. Dean Anderson. Copyright © 2010 John Wiley & Sons

Figure 51 - Levels of Change Commitment and Communication

6.4. The Art of Body Language

Art of Body Language as a key factor in effective communications.

6.4.1. Background

Albert Mehrabian, a pioneer researcher of body language in the 1950s found that the total impact of a message is:

- 7% verbal (words only)
- 38% vocal (including tone of voice, inflection and other sounds)
- 55% non-verbal (body language)

Body language includes facial expressions, body movement, gestures, eye contact, posture, tone of voice, and even muscle tension and breathing. The sending and receiving of body language signals happens at both conscious and unconscious levels.

6.4.2. Understanding and Using Body Language

Body Language (technically known as *kinesics*) is an important dimension of communications. You need to be aware about what your non-verbal cues are saying, and be careful to ensure that your body language is consistent with and emphasizes the verbal message you are trying to convey. Equally, you need to be aware of what others non-verbal cues are saying—how they shape what they are trying to communicate, or how they are reacting to what you are saying. Body language encompasses:

- How we position our bodies
- Our closeness to and the space between us and other people
- Facial expressions
- Eye movement and focus
- How we touch ourselves and others
- How our bodies connect with other objects
- Breathing and other unconscious bodily functions such as heartbeat and perspiration

You can enhance your ability to communicate effectively by using open body language:

- Arms uncrossed
- Standing with an open stance
- Sitting on the edge of your seat
- Maintaining eye contact

To improve your non-verbal skills:

- Practice observing how others use body language can help you learn to better receive and use nonverbal signals
- Be aware of cultural differences—people from different cultures sometimes use different nonverbal communication
- Look at nonverbal communication signals collectively—don't read too much into a single gesture or nonverbal cue
- Use nonverbal signals that match your words—nonverbal communication should reinforce what is being said, not contradict it

- Adjust your nonverbal signals according to the context
- Use body language to convey positive feelings
- Use positive body language to signal confidence—stand tall, shoulders back, smiling, maintaining eye contact, and delivering a firm handshake

6.5. The Art of Emotional Intelligence

6.5.1. Background

Emotional intelligence (EI) refers to the ability to perceive, assess, and control emotions. Some researchers suggest that EI can be learned and strengthened, while others claim it is an inborn characteristic.

6.5.2. Elements of Emotional Intelligence

Travis Bradberry and Jean Greaves, in their excellent book, *Emotional Intelligence 2.0*, with corresponding website and online Emotional Intelligence Appraisal at http://www.talentsmart.com/ describe four skills that comprise Emotional Intelligence:

- Self-awareness
- Self-management
- Social awareness
- Relationship management

The first two skills are related to personal competence, and the second two are related to social competence.

Emotional Intelligence requires an awareness of what you and others are thinking and feeling as they communicate, including:

- Understanding and empathizing with what is really troubling other people
- Understanding yourself, including what's really troubling you and what you really want
- Staying motivated to understand and empathize with the person you're interacting with, even if you don't like them or their message
- Communicating clearly and effectively, even when delivering negative messages
- Building strong, trusting, and rewarding relationships, thinking creatively, solve problems, and resolve conflicts

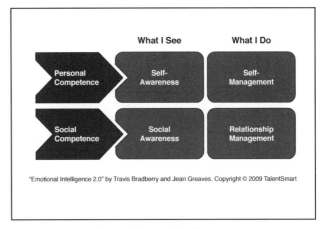

"Emotional Intelligence 2.0" by Travis Bradberry and Jean Greaves. Copyright © 2009 TalentSmart

Figure 52 - The Four Skills of Emotional Intelligence

6.6. The Art of Listening

6.6.1. Background

Most of us sincerely believe that we listen effectively, so we don't think we need to develop our listening skills. But, in reality, very few of use listening effectively. In our eagerness to show people we are smart, understand their needs and can help them, we often fail to really listen to what they are saying—or, more importantly, what they mean and why they mean that. Successful listening means not just understanding the words or the information being communicated, but also understanding how the speaker feels about what they're communicating.

6.6.2. Effective Listening

Research shows that effective listening increases the amount and quality of information you get from the people with whom you communicate, increases others' trust in you, reduces conflict, and increases your ability to influence and motivate others. Effective listening means actively absorbing the information given to you by a speaker, showing that you are listening and interested in what they are trying to communicate, and providing feedback to the speaker so that they know the message was received as intended.

Effective listening:

- Makes the speaker feel heard and understood—helps build a deeper connection
- Creates an environment where everyone feels safe to express ideas, opinions, and feelings
- Saves time by helping clarify information, avoiding conflict and misunderstanding
- Relieves negative emotions when the speaker feels that he or she has been truly heard

6.6.3. Six Steps to Effective Listening

1. *Be present.* If you can, be physically with the people with whom you are communicating. Face the speaker and maintain eye contact (but without staring, which can make people uncomfortable). If you can't be physically with them, it is even more important to be present—don't be distracted or fall into the contemporary trap of mutli-tasking. You may not have the chance to hear what they are trying to communicate again. Even worse, if they sense you are not really listening, you will erode trust and weaken the relationship irreparably. Relax, and focus on the speaker. If you are physically present, show your attentiveness through your body language. Nod or use other gestures to encourage them to continue, show that you are listening and understanding what is being said.

2. *Stop talking.* Mark Twain famously said, "If we were meant to talk more than we listen, we would have two mouths and one ear." Listen to what others are saying, without interrupting them, talking over them or finishing their sentences. Be comfortable with silence. Introverts need time to process their thoughts before they speak—give them that time. Extroverts tend to think out loud to process their thoughts. The first words out of their mouth might not make sense, or convey what they really are trying to say—give them time to get to the point. A pause does not necessarily mean that the speaker has finished. Be patient and let them continue at their own pace. Wait for the speaker to finish their thought before responding or asking clarifying questions. Focus on what the speaker is saying. Try not to think about what you are going to say next.

3. *Listen to the tone being used.* Volume and tone both add information to what someone is communicating. Good speakers use volume and tone to shape what they are trying to say.

4. *Validate understanding.* If you are unsure what they are really saying, ask clarifying questions. If you think you have understood them, summarize back to them what you think you heard, in your own words.

5. *Empathize.* Try to understand the other person's point of view and what they are feeling. Let go of preconceived ideas and have an open mind. If the speaker says something that you disagree with, wait and construct your response, but keep an open mind to the views and opinions of others.

6. *Listen for the ideas behind the words.* What are they really trying to communicate and why? But don't jump to conclusions—validate by asking questions or by communicating back in your own words what you think they really mean. Be aware of and use the Ladder of Inference to get behind the words.

6.6.4. The Ladder of Inference

When we communicate, we infer things from the messages being conveyed. These inferences, the conclusions we reach from them and the actions we take based upon them are frequently wrong! The Ladder of Inference, illustrated in Figure 53, is a way of understanding the thinking process we typically (and subconsciously!) follow to get from facts to decisions and actions.

The stages of inference are:

1. I see reality and facts in observable data and through my own experiences.

2. I filter the reality and facts to create a selected reality.

3. I create an interpreted reality by adding my own meanings to the selected reality.

4. I make assumptions about the interpreted reality.

5. I draw conclusions based on my assumptions.

6. Over time, I adopt beliefs about the world around me—these beliefs impact what I observe (step 1), how I select from what I observe (step 2) and how I interpet these selected, observed or experience facts.

7. The actions I take are based upon the beliefs I have adopted over time.

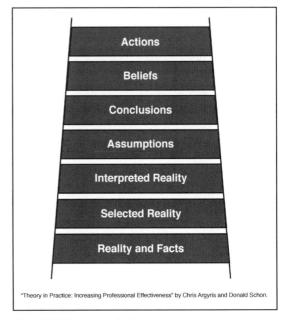

"Theory in Practice: Increasing Professional Effectiveness" by Chris Argyris and Donald Schon.

Figure 53 - The Ladder of Inference

It is no wonder that communications is so fraught with misunderstanding and false assumptions! The Ladder of Inference can be used to surface the indisputable facts, the belief systems through which we interpret those facts, and the assumptions we make by challenging ourselves and others to think through:

· Is the conclusion valid?

· What assumptions are we making, why are we making them and are they valid?

· Why are we drawing these conclusion?

· Are our conclusion really based on all the facts?

· Why do we believe what we do?

6.7. The Art of Rhetoric and Persuasion

the characteristics of powerful rhetoric and the science of persuasion, and how to strengthen your ability to present ideas to and influence others.

6.7.1. Background

Although the term *rhetoric* has taken on some negative connotations over the last century, it used to be considered one of the *high arts*. Aristotle expounded on the elements of powerful rhetoric around 350 B.C.

6.7.2. The Three Components of Powerful Rhetoric

Aristotle argued (and contemporary research has validated) that powerful communications contains three types of proofs—Ethical Proofs (*Ethos*), Logical Proofs (*Logos*) and Emotional Proofs (*Pathos*), as illustrated in Figure 54.

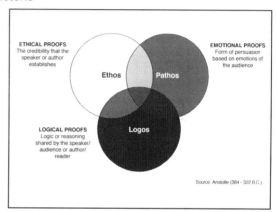

Ethical Proofs

The author's character that gives value to his words. Ethical Proofs Comprises:

- Intelligence is indicated by a certain amount of knowledge of the subject.

- Common sense combined with convincing arguments that are logical is essential in demonstrating this quality.

- Discussing the various viewpoints of a subject also exhibits a certain amount of intelligence.

Figure 54 - Rhetorical Proofs

- The audience consists of as many opinions as people and therefore, recognizing these viewpoints only helps the author in building his persuasion.

- Virtue and good character is another quality by which the author becomes believable.

- Stating ones beliefs, values, and priorities in connection with the subject assists in convincing the audience of the argument.

- If these beliefs and values coincide with the majority of the audience, the writer is well on his way to success.

- Goodwill is the last attribute essential to establishing credibility. This characteristic projects concerns for the audience's viewpoint and respects their intelligence, sincerity and commonsense.

Logical Proofs

Logos meant more in ancient Greek than logic or reasoning, it meant "thought plus action." In other words, it is fully credible that the idea you are arguing for would be valid and reasonable if you acted on it.

Emotional Proofs

Emotional Proofs appeal to the emotions by arousing feelings of pity, sympathy, tenderness, or sorrow.

6.7.3. Communicating to Influence and Persuade

Practice including Ethical, Logical and Emotional Proofs in your written and spoken communications as well as in your formal presentations. Look back over your writings and presentations and determine to which degree the the Proofs were present.

6.7.4. The Science of Persuasion

In their wonderful YouTube video, "Secrets from the Science of Persuasion," Dr. Robert Cialdini and Steve Martin describe 6 key principles of persuasion:

- *Reciprocity*—give in order to receive
- *Scarcity*—what is unique in your proposal, what do they stand to lose if they don't accept it?
- *Authority*—signal what makes you a credible authority to be making your proposal?
- *Consistency*—ask for small initial commitments—voluntary, active, public, ideally, in writing.
- *Liking*—people who are similar to us, who pay us sincere compliments, who cooperate with us towards mutual goals.
- *Consensus*—show that others are doing what you are proposing.

6.8. Influencing and Persuading

Influencing and Persuading is a technique used to help you achieve a result you want through indirect means when you lack the power or formal authority to get it directly, or when you have the power and choose not to use it.

6.8.1. Background

BRMs typically work through influence rather than direct authority—both with their Business Partners and with the Provider organization. As such, they must be masters of the skills of influence and persuasion.

- Persuasion implies convincing another person through the strength of one's argument—the logical and emotional impact of one's language—sometimes in conversation, sometimes in writing or other media, but almost always through the use of words directed at others.
- Influence describes one's broader impact on people and situations and can be either verbal or non-verbal means; influence includes, but is not limited to, persuasion.

In the BRM role, influence most often means the ability to affect a stakeholder's point of view, decisions, actions or accomplishments. The need for influence shows up most commonly when that other person is a decision maker in areas that impact IT activities, and especially if the decisions being made are on the critical path for an IT strategy, architecture, project or other prior commitment.

In these cases the stakeholder may be on the supply side of things—for example, a colleague in IT, a vendor contracted to provide IT services or a key member of an industry standards group. Or that decision maker may be someone on the demand side—a business unit or financial executive, a manager leading a function using IT services, a third party service Provider contracted by the business unit, or even another firm upstream or downstream in the supply chain with whom information exchange and systems compatibility or inter-operability are important.

Influence skills also come into play in another context—shaping the course of business events at which decisions are made, where the BRM is just one of many players, all seeking to exert or resist influence. In the course of a typical week in the role, every Business Partner participates in numerous such events. Examples might include a planning meeting, progress review, feasibility study, strategy session, team meeting on alternatives approaches, working sessions to design, plan, budget or problem-solve in relation to a specific initiative.

The common characteristic for the BRM in both cases—the need to shape individual behavior and the need to shape events—is that he or she lacks the power, authority or clout to make things happen. Instead it's only through indirect means that one can make a difference. And that's where influence comes into play.

For that reason some would argue that the ability to influence is the most important part of the BRM role; for others, influence merely supports the many other skills required in the role. But whatever the case, BRMs are likely to find themselves using influence every day, in many ways—setting direction, shaping demand, shaping supply, evaluating results, and most important when addressing and resolving differences of opinion between dependent parties.

6.8.2. Purpose

The influence techniques included here, while applicable across a variety of situations are primarily intended for use in issue resolution—dealing with the inevitable problems, disagreements and breakdowns that show up in the course of getting things done. The reason is straightforward—those are the situations in which people are most likely to forget what we've learned from prior experience about what to say, and how to say it, to be persuasive. Instead, in many problem solving situations where there are major differences of opinion, we tend to rely on the forcefulness of argument—talking more, pushing harder (or getting more defensive), and in general letting our emotions take over—especially when the pressure is on, expectations are high, deadlines loom and management is looking for results *yesterday*.

The fact is, we all learn basic influence skills in early childhood; having no power or authority, it's only through influence that we get what we need or want, through influence that we navigate family life and build our relationships with siblings and parents, and later with friends, teachers and other authority figures.

But the BRM, dealing with tough problems and surrounded by worthy adversaries, is likely to find those informal influencing skills falling short. The situations we're called on to influence are more complicated, with more variables, than what we've encountered in private life. In addition, we have too much at stake and things happen too fast—we need to develop industrial strength influencing skills because, in spite of best intentions, our prior skill level is not good enough.

BRM's are not alone in facing this challenge; we can draw on the collective wisdom of successful influencers in other settings—professionals, leaders and managers in similar roles—and seek to emulate best practices they've developed. The approaches, step-by-step procedures and techniques described below were selected to give BRM's a place to start thinking. Based on external best practice, they're designed to focus attention on a few key components of influence, beginning with a simple but powerful depiction of the Influence Process in four phases (see Figure 55).

6.8.3. The Influence Process

There are four major steps to the process of influencing an individual or a group—Framing the conversations appropriately, structuring the Dialogs within that frame, Enrolling the key stakeholders who will be needed to convert influence into organizational outcomes and, if necessary, re-setting the frame.

6.8.4. Framing the Conversations

Framing is defining the issue at hand in terms both parties, or multiple participants in an event, can agree on. Framing, as a pre-cursor to the problem-solving discussion, allows you (the influencer) to work out your own position in advance, before getting caught up in the emotion of debate. The ideas is to frame your going-in proposition as follows:

- All parties share a common goal or objective
- Current reality falls short of what's required to achieve that goal
- There are multiple interpretations—multiple stories to explain why
- Each party needs to acknowledge the other's story … no pre-judgment
- Only then can we can explore causes and commit to fixes

Think carefully about each component of your message, to be clear about what you're planning to say, once the dialog begins, as well as where you want input from the other person in order to understand fully their side of the story.

Business Relationship Management Institute

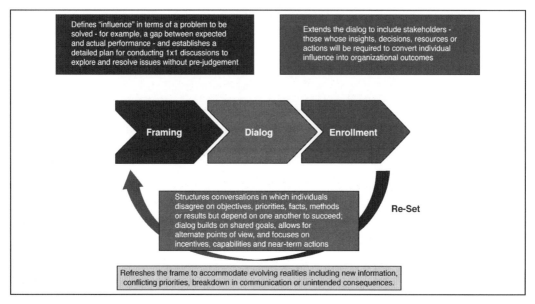

Figure 55 - The Influence Process

Shared Goals or Concerns

In your planning, as well as in the conversation itself, begin by establishing common ground between the two of you. Outline and be prepared to describe what you think are the most relevant shared goals or concerns, those that will appeal on an emotional level to the person you're trying to influence as well as representing your own intentions and commitments. If you gravitate to shared goals, articulate them in personally meaningful ways rather than at an abstract level or in terms of corporate jargon. If you're highlighting concerns, be specific about what's at stake: Is it a specific outcome or oversight? A series of problems that you suspect have a common cause? A relationship that's not working well? Choose your focus carefully and work on your wording—what you'll say and how you'll say it—to maximize the likelihood that the other person will agree with you. That way, in case the other topics are more controversial and you need to re-group, you'll have established some high ground as a place to retreat and re-group.

Truth about Today

Any problem or issue can be described in terms of current reality, based on the facts of the situation. But in framing your message, it's more effective to begin with past commitments, expectations or plans—assuming they were agreed to by both parties—and then putting forward the facts on the ground. In that way you focus attention on the gap—plan vs. actual, promised vs. delivered, expected vs. observed—in a way that leads easily to an investigation into that gap, and ultimately to trial solutions.

My Point of View

Assuming you've mastered your *story* and minimized the associated evaluation and attribution of responsibility, this is where you can outline your interpretations and opinions about the problem. The best way to proceed here is to be tentative rather than definitive, "From what I can see, it seems like X … How do you see it?" That approach allows for the other person to enter into the discussion openly and minimizes defensiveness or avoidance.

Your Point of View

The challenge here is to take the other person's point of view as your starting point. What would he or she say in expressing their interpretations and opinions in regard to the same problem? Developing this *what if* scenario will help you appreciate the other person's position, anticipate points of pain and even discover some alternate truth that would lead you to further modify your own opinions.

Constraints and Limitations

List possible explanations for the gap described above—shortage of resources, lack of information, inadequate design—being honest with yourself as to constraints on your side, and as thorough as possible

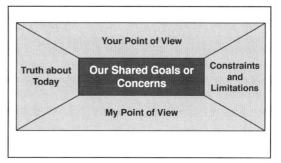

Figure 56 - Framing Your Message So As To Be Heard

identifying possible limitations on the other side. Once again, you're trying to anticipate what will be discussed and minimize the risk of unexpected excuses. Distinguish minor constraints from major impediments, and for the latter consider who could potentially alleviate them—as candidates for more influencing down the road.

6.8.5. Dialog

Using a structured approach to issue resolution in a one-on-one conversation with key decision makers or opinion leaders. In this step two parties deal with the content outlined above, with special attention to three critical points in the conversation:

- Setup—the first few minutes, to establish common ground
- Wrap-up—the last few minutes, to clarify post-meeting commitments
- Check-up—potential flash points, to get the conversation back on track

6.8.6. Enrollment

Using a structured approach to influence a broader audience across the organization—e.g. engaging key stakeholders in planning, decision-making or implementation. As multiple parties are involved this phase extends beyond personal influence to include systemic elements:

- Establishing a case for action and seeking out early adopters
- Describing an ideal solution and a roadmap for getting there
- Removing obstacles at the front line; taking ground with quick wins
- Building momentum and demonstrating success at each step

6.8.7. Re-set

Anticipating that influence will not always be successful the first time around and being prepared for mid-course corrections, based on feedback from key stakeholders—Business Partners, suppliers, management or one's own team members and colleagues.

6.9. Expressing a Unique Value Proposition

Expressing a Unique Value Proposition is a technique for positioning an offer or opportunity with your Business Partner and Provider colleagues in a way that is clear, compelling and convincing.

Expressing a Unique Value Proposition is a framework to help BRMs craft a clear, compelling and convincing *value proposition*. The technique can be used very effectively when expressing the value of your role as a BRM. It comprises four elements:

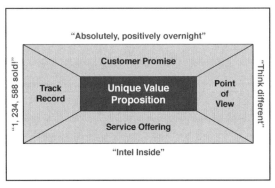

Figure 57 - Expressing a unique Value Proposition

Customer Promise

What are you promising your Business Partner? Why should they engage with you and invest their time with you? How will you help them achieve their goals? What commitments are you making to them? Think about the crisp customer promise that Federal Express made when it first appeared on the scene— "Absolutely, positively overnight!" In three simple words, FedEx was telling you exactly why and when you need them and what value you could count on when you used them.

Track Record

Why should your Business Partner believe you? What history do you have that supports your value proposition? Do you have credible testimonials from others who the Business Partner respects and trusts? If not, how are you going to establish that track record—what actions will you take to earn those testimonials?

Service Offering

How would you brand the service you provide? What is unique about your personal brand and your services that creates an appropriate image in your Business Partner's mind? The label "Intel Inside" is interpreted by millions to represent quality, power, innovation, and an implied *standard*—if it has that badge, all software will run on it flawlessly. If you left your mark or *label* on your contributions to the Business Partner, what would you like that mark to stand for? Why should your Business Partner care about your brand—what's in it for them?

Point of View

What strongly held points of view do you hold that should be of interest to your Business Partner? Are you simply going to deliver whatever your Business Partner wants from you? Or do you hold certain beliefs about, for example, the scarcity of resources and therefore the need to see significant business value in a request in order to act on it? Do you believe in strictly adhering to policies and guidelines, or do you believe flexibility is important, and would sooner "ask forgiveness than permission?"

Crafting a Unique Value Proposition

The value proposition must ultimately address all four elements above. How you communicate those elements may vary based upon the audience and circumstances, and your value proposition will change over time, but you should take the time to think through the elements and start working on your value proposition as soon as you can. Test it with colleagues and mentors. Refine it as you learn more about your Business Partner needs and expectation and as you learn more about your abilities as a BRM through practice.

Page Intentionally Left Blank

Chapter 6

Afterword

I hope that you found the information within these pages to be helpful to you, as you went through your training and took your BRMP certification exam with confidence. We also hope this information will be something of a handbook for you in your work and as you develop your career.

Your BRMP certification is a significant achievement, but please don't look at it as the end of a process, but rather consider it an important milestone, a beginning of the next exciting phase in your career journey.

If you are not a BRMI member yet, please consider joining us and hundreds of BRMs accross the world now! Let us help you develop further and support you through your journey. As a BRMI member you are part of an important professional community. You will gain immediate access to a rich and growing portfolio of expertly designed professional development and collaboration resources. These unique tools will help you address the many challenging questions your role might be facing today and significantly enhance your ability to deliver maximum value to your organization.

If you are already a BRMI member, we hope you will be an active member in our vibrant community—forging relationships around the world and participating in the growth of the BRM profession. Perhaps, you will become a BRMiBOK author—helping to expand the documented knowledge for your professional colleagues. Perhaps, you will become a BRMiBOK curator, with the ultimate accountability for the quality of pages within a given knowledge domain. Perhaps, you would like to deliver or co-deliver one or more of our monthly member webinars—teaching is one of the best routes to learning and sharing your insights and experiences is highly satisfying and rewarding. Perhaps, you have an ambition to become a trainer? We can help connect you with Accredited Training Organizations and get you started on the path towards becoming a BRMI trainer. Thank you very much!

I wish you well on your journey and hope that you will be in touch!

Sincerely,
Dr. Aleksandr Zhuk
Co-Founder and President
Business Relationship Management Institute

7. List of Figures

8.   Glossary of Terms

Term	Definition
BOK Frameworks	A BOK Framework is a useful model or skeleton of interlinked items that is applied in one or more places in the BRM Body of Knowledge to provide insight into why things are the way they are, how they could be improved, and/or how to effect change.
BRM Core Disciplines	BRM Core Disciplines are defined as part of the House of BRM. They represent the patterns of behavior that the role, discipline and organizational capability of Business Relationship Management must exhibit.
BRM Core Themes	BRM Core Themes are central topics that run throughout the Business Relationship Management (BRM) role, discipline and organizational capability.
BRM Metaphors	The metaphors for Business Relationship Management (Connector, Orchestrator and Navigator) can be helpful ways to think about and describe the BRM role, discipline and organizational capability.
BRM-Related Standards	The BRM role is referenced in several industry standards, mostly associated with Information Technology, Service Management and the IT Profession. These include ITIL, COBIT, ISO/IEC 20000-1:2011, and the SFIA skills framework.
BRMI Provider Capability Model	To understand BRM requires putting BRM in the context of a Provider Capability Model; therefore, the purpose of the BRMI Provider Capability Model is to represent all the capabilities typically required of a Provider (e.g. IT organization, HR organization, combination of insourced and outsourced capabilities, etc.) to effectively address the demand for the Provider's products and services by the business. This model is intentionally generalized to represent any type of shared service (like IT, HR, or Finance) or any external Provider for that matter, so some capabilities may be more meaningful for one type of Provider than another. Each capability in the model "explodes" into a more detailed model
Building a Customer Value Hierarchy	The Customer Value Hierarchy (CVH) is a technique for discovering the needs and value expectations of an individual Business Partner. Used correctly, it allows the Account Team to not only identify the specific needs of the Business Partner, but also to categorize those needs into three levels of criticality.
Building a Relationship Improvement Plan	The Relationship Improvement Plan is typically used after Building a Customer Value Hierarchy and Diagnosing Relationship Quality techniques have been used as part of the Strategic Relationship Management process

Term	Definition
Building a Relationship Strategy on a Page	The Relationship Strategy on a Page (RSOAP) is used by BRMs and their Account Teams. As with Building a Customer Value Hierarchy, the value in this technique is the process of completing it rather than the completed form itself. In this page, we describe the content and structure of the RSOAP, and suggest an approach for completing it.
Building Trust Relationships	Building Trust Relationships describes the elements, principles and process to build trust relationships between the Business Partner and Provider. At the higher levels of Business Relationship Maturity, trust relationships are vital enablers to shape high quality demand and deliver on the promise of value. The BRM needs to be aware and understand what it takes to build and sustain these trust relationships.
Business Capability Roadmapping	Business Capability Roadmapping is an approach to aligning Business and IT strategies and imperatives.
Business Outcomes	Business Outcomes are a means to establishing a discipline of value—from clarifying an opportunity, through to managing scope, establishing focus and ownership, through to measuring and optimizing realized value.
Business Partner	Business Partner is the term we use to refer to the individual(s) that the Business Relationship Manager represents on behalf of the Provider organization.
Business Partner's Decision Cycle	The Business Partner's Decision Cycle is a useful way to understand, assess and improve the nature of the Business Partner-Provider relationship
Business Relationship Manager	A Business Relationship Manager (BRM) is a role that serves as the strategic interface between a Provider (e.g. IT Organization) and one or more Business Partners to stimulate, surface and shape business demand for the Provider's products and services and ensure that the potential business value from those products and services is captured, realized, optimized and recognized.
Business Relationship Maturity Model	The Business Relationship Maturity Model (BRMM) is a way to help surface and understand the maturity of the relationship between a Provider (e.g. internal IT organization) and their Business Partner.
Business Transition Management Capability Model	A Business Transition Management Capability Model describes the key Capabilities necessary to clarify, motivate, orchestrate, drive, sustain and monitor major business transition.
Business Transition Management Explained	Business Transition Management (BTM) is a deliberate approach for managing the human dynamics before, during and after implementing a business change initiative in order to prevent *business value leakage*.

Term	Definition
Business Value Leakage	Business Value Leakage occurs when the full Potential Value from solving a business problem or exploiting an opportunity is not realized in practice. Value leaks when the Value System between Provider and Business Partner is misaligned; when opportunities to create value are missed, when Provider solutions fail to fully meet the needs of the opportunity, when the solution is deployed or operated in a suboptimal way, or when business value measurement, accountability or organizational capability are lacking.
Business-IT Governance	Business-IT Governance describes the framework of decision rights and accountabilities and the structures and policies that support that framework to encourage desired behavior to realize maximum value from information technology. It formalizes how business makes decisions about the deployment and delivery of IT throughout the enterprise.
Business-Provider Alignment	The Business-Provider Alignment Model helps to understand and analyze the four key elements of alignment—business environment, strategic context, Provider strategy and Provider investment portfolio. It illustrates the *barriers* that typically surround these elements and impede alignment.
Business-Provider Maturity Model	The Business-Provider Maturity Model is a way to help surface and understand the growth in maturity of business demand for Provider services and capabilities, and a Provider organization's maturity of supply capabilities needed to both satisfy and shape that demand.
Capability	A Capability is everything it takes, both visible and behind the scenes, that makes producing a good or providing a service possible. This includes having people with the right competencies to play the roles required by defined processes, and armed with useful techniques and tools, all backed by management systems that create incentives for performance and improvement.
COBIT	COBIT provides managers, auditors, and IT users with a set of generally accepted measures, indicators, processes and best practices, to assist them in improving the benefits derived through the use of information technology, and developing appropriate IT governance and control in a company.
Competency	A Competency is an identifiable and standardized set of skills and experience that are required for an individual to effectively perform a specific role or collection of roles.
Components of the Business Case	A Business Case is used to clarify the nature of a proposed investment and the cost and benefits of making that investment. It is used prior to making an investment to determine if that investment should be made, and after the investment has been made to determine if the value forecasted from the investment has been realized.

Term	Definition
Concepts	A Concept is an idea, abstraction, or generalization derived or inferred from examples and can help shape a shared understanding.
Content Types	A Content Type is a type of knowledge that has value in being represented consistently from one instance to another. For example: Business Analyst and Program Manager are both examples of Roles. While they are different Roles to be sure, it adds value to be consistent in the way both Roles are defined (and all other Roles for that matter). That makes Role a Content Type in the BRMiBOK.
Core Values	Core Values form the foundation on which we perform our work and conduct ourselves. Core values tend to be stable over time. They shape how interact with each other and how we go about our work. They are the practices we use (or should be using) every day in everything we do. Core Values are best *discovered* naturally, rather than imposed. Organizations with high maturity in Human Relations practices often hire based upon an individual's core values, believing it is easier to develop someone's competencies than it is to shape their core values.
Creating a Mission Statement	This is a technique for creating a Mission Statement - a formal, concise, written statement of the purpose of an organization. It is typically one aspect of an organization's Vision.
Creating a Vision Statement	This is a technique for creating a Vision Statement - a vivid and idealized description of what an organization wants to be which inspires and energizes people within the organization. A Vision Statement is one aspect of a Vision, but is not the same as a Vision. A Vision goes well beyond a Vision Statement and typically includes aspects such as a Mission Statement, Values, Long term stretch goals, and sometimes Principles.
Customer Experience	Customer Experience (CX) is an important concept for Business Relationship Management. Not to be confused with Customer Satisfaction, CX has been defined as "The customer's rational and emotional responses across the entire process of accomplishing one or more goals."
Customer Relationship Management	Customer Relationship Management (CRM) is a source of many of the techniques and disciplines of Business Relationship Management (BRM). However, while CRM most often refers to a company's external customers, the BRM typically deals with a company's internal customers for an internal Provider's products and/or services.
Demand Shaping	Demand Shaping (sometimes referred to as *Demand Management*) is the process by which possibilities for using the Provider's services within the business are surfaced and capitalized upon. The goal is to identify that set of possibilities that will create the most value for the organization.

Term	Definition
Developing Principles to Resolve Choices Among Compelling Alternatives	This is a technique for developing a Principle—a meaningful description of a code of conduct or desired organizational behavior. Principles provide clarity of intent or purpose around otherwise contentious issues. Principles guide decision-making, particularly when decisions involve otherwise equally compelling alternatives.
Diagnosing Relationship Quality	The Diagnosing Relationship Quality technique helps determine the strength of a BRMs relationship with their Business Partner.
Diagnosing Resistance or Influence Issues	Diagnosing Resistance or Influence Issues is a technique designed to help develop a hypothesis regarding behaviors you have observed which appear to have contributed to a behavior problem and review possible reasons for that behavior by suggesting six possible reasons someone might have acted in the ways you observed, or failed to act in the way you would have wanted to see. The diagnostic can also be used to help understand sources of resistance to change.
Effective BRM Communications	Effective BRM Communications covers a number of important Business Relationship Management skills needed to effectively communicate and manage expectations, and to drive results.
Expressing a Unique Value Proposition	Expressing a Unique Value Proposition is a technique for positioning an offer or opportunity with your Business Partner and Provider colleagues in a way that is clear, compelling and convincing.
Framework for the BRM Competency Model	A Competency Model is a tool to describe, assess and develop the knowledge, skills and behaviors generally needed for successful performance in a given role. Organizations use Competency Models in many ways. They may use them to help describe the type of competencies they want in candidates they are considering hiring. Or, they may use them to assess the performance of employees and provide them a framework for future development. Other uses include considering what type and level of ability is needed from someone to successfully perform in a specific level job or perform a process or contribute to a project.
Framework for the BRMI Provider Capability Model	The BRMI Provider Capability Model uses a Capability Model framework to represent a set of related capabilities that is an extension of a Value Chain Analysis approach popularized by Michael Porter. Our model represents the major capabilities any organization would need to have in place where there is a business generating demand for products and services and a Provider trying to meet that demand. Our framework also uses the technique of decomposition, which allows each higher-level capability to serve as the context for a more granular set of capabilities. The decomposition progresses down until the underlying Processes are discovered at the lowest level of decomposition. In this way, the reader can progress from a higher abstraction of capability to a lower level of abstraction as needed with a clear understanding of the context of each capability.

Term	Definition
House of BRM	The House of BRM is a graphical representation intended to convey key aspects of a successful Business Relationship Management role, discipline and organizational capability.
Implementing the Strategic Relationship Management Process	The Strategic Relationship Management Process is used by Providers to manage their key Business Partner relationships.
Influencing and Persuading	Influencing and Persuading is a technique used to help you achieve a result you want through indirect means when you lack the power or formal authority to get it directly, or when you have the power and choose not to use it.
ISO/IEC 20000	ISO/IEC 20000-1:2011 is a service management system (SMS) standard. It specifies requirements for the service provider to plan, establish, implement, operate, monitor, review, maintain and improve an SMS. The requirements include the design, transition, delivery and improvement of services to fulfill agreed service requirements.*
IT Engagement Model	The IT Engagement Model was developed by Nils O. Fonstad at MIT's Center for Information Systems Research to describe the linking mechanisms important to business-IT Engagement.
ITIL	ITIL (IT Infrastructure Library) is an approach to IT Service Management that embodies a framework for identifying, planning, delivering and supporting IT services to the business.
ITIL Business Relationship Management	ITIL approaches Business Relationship Management from a Service Management perspective rather than from the perspective of strategic business value. This orients the BRM role, discipline and organizational capability towards a lower maturity Provider, where Service Management disciplines are not in place or are weak.
Linking Business Drivers With Technology	This technique links a Business Partner's Business Drivers with Technology and illustrates the distinctions between Solution Based and Value Based discussions between a Provider and their Business Partner.
Metrics	A Metric is any type of measurement used to gauge some quantifiable component of an organization's current performance or forecast of future performance.
Organizational Clarity	Clarity of organizational mission, vision, roles, responsibilities, processes and decision rights is particularly important for leaders of Provider organizations today as Provider management and operational roles are increasingly dispersing throughout the business rather than being performed within a homogeneous Provider organization.

Term	Definition
Portfolio Balancing	Portfolio Balancing is a technique that ensures that amounts invested in different Portfolio Asset classes are balanced given the business strategy.
Portfolio Classification	Two methods of Portfolio Classification for an Information Technology investment portfolio. Once a classification scheme has been defined and agreed, target investment and return levels can be set for each investment and subsequently tracked.
Portfolio Management Explained	Portfolio Management is a central mechanism for Value Management. The term 'portfolio management' is often abused—for example, a 'laundry list' of projects is referred to as a portfolio. This is a very dangerous abuse of Portfolio Management concepts and techniques and Business Relationship Management must work hard to position Portfolio Management properly.
Principle	A Principle is a meaningful description of a code of conduct or desired organizational behavior. Principles provide clarity of intent or purpose around otherwise contentious issues. Principles encourage consistency in behavior of IT resources across the enterprise. Most importantly, Principles guide decision-making, particularly when decisions involve otherwise equally compelling alternatives.
Process	A Process outlines a structured set of activities designed to accomplish a specific objective. A process takes one or more defined inputs and turns them into defined outputs. A process may reference any of the roles, responsibilities, tools and management controls required to reliably deliver the outputs. Processes describe *what* to do whereas Techniques specify *how* to do it.
Process Management	Process Management refers to a set of disciplines and techniques for planning, monitoring and improving the performance of a process.
Provider	Provider is the term we use to describe the organization that the Business Relationship Manager represents to their Business Partner. The most common type of Provider organization that has a formally established BRM role is Information Technology, but BRMs are increasingly deployed in other service providers, such as Human Resources, Finance, Facilities, Training, etc.
Publication	A Publication is a book, article, or other published piece of content related to the discipline of business relationship management.
RACI Charting	A RACI Chart is a matrix of responsibilities that is especially useful in clarifying "who is supposed to do what" across an organizational setting. A RACI chart can be used to establish clear accountability for the performance of a process, or clear accountability for the making of a decision.

Term	Definition
Relationship Value Mapping	Relationship Value Mapping is a technique used in conjunction with the Diagnosing Relationship Quality and Relationship Improvement Planning techniques as part of the Strategic Relationship Management process.
Roles	In the context of an Operating Model, a Role defines the competencies and background required or expected of a person in order for that person to be success in the performance of a related set of processes. This page lists common roles in an IT Provider that have important relationships with the BRM role.
Service Management	Service Management embodies a number of disciplines used to optimize service-intensive supply chains. These disciplines include Strategic Service Management, Service Strategy and Customer Management. One special application is IT Service Management which includes the International Standard ISO/IEC 20000 and the ITIL Framework.
SFIA	The Skills Framework for the Information Age (SFIA) is a system for IT Professionals to match the Skills of the workforce to the requirements of the business. It is a logical two-dimensional skills framework defined by areas of work on one axis and levels of responsibility on the other. It has been proven as an effective resource that benefits business by facilitating all aspects of the management of capability in corporate and educational environments.
Skill	A Skill is a specific and desirable expertise that when combined with other skills can create a Competency in an individual.
Strategic Relationship Management	Strategic Relationship Management is used by BRMs and their teams to manage their key Business Partner relationships.
Strategic versus Tactical BRM	Comparison of the Strategic and Tactical BRM role variations. The former operates in the context of business strategy and Provider initiatives intended to enact business strategy. The latter tends to operate in the context of Service Management and is primarily concerned with steady state services.
Strategy and Operating Model Components and Linkages	A Provider Strategy describes the Provider Mission, Vision, Strategic Intents, Outcomes, Values, Principles, and Policies. A Provider Operating Model is an abstract representation of how an enterprise manages its Provider resources and assets in order to deliver against its Strategy, including Governance, Services, Processes, Organization and Metrics. The linkage between these Strategy and Operating Model components are important to the Provider's ability to deliver business value.

Term	Definition
The BRM and Internal Markets	An Internal Market brings the logic of a market system and free enterprise into an organization. In this context, Business Relationship Management acts as a channel between Providers and purchasers of products and services.
The Cliff Analogy for Change	The Cliff Analogy can be helpful in explaining stakeholders and transition leaders the way people typically perceive major change and how to approach change so as to maximize the probability of success and minimize the stress of the transition process.
Types of Relationship and Types of Business Partner	Business Partner behavior with regard to their Relationship Manager will typically vary based upon the types of activity in play at any given point in time. It is unrealistic to expect a Strategic Relationship for all relationship activities.
Useful BRM Metaphors	Useful BRM Metaphors include Navigator, Connector, and Orchestrator. For more on these metaphors, please see BRM Metaphors.
Value Creation	Value creation is a commonly used term, but a very slippery concept. It is generally said to be the primary aim of any business. Customers buy products or services because they experience some sort of value from them. In turn, the suppliers of those products or services create value for shareholders in the form of increased share price or stock dividends.
Value Management	Value Management ties together into an holistic and comprehensive approach the concepts of Ideation, Value Planning, Portfolio Management and the Business Case to capture, optimize and communicate the business value of Provider investments and capabilities.

Page Intentionally Left Blank